MW01542060

MAKING DISCIPLES

**A Rationale For Making
Disciples Of Jesus Christ
And A Practical Guide To Meet With Others
One-on-One To Make
Mature Disciples of Jesus Christ
Who Make More
Mature Disciples of Jesus Christ.**

**By
PJ Bogoniewski**

Making Disciples

© 2016, Rev. James E. Bogoniewski, Jr.

All Rights Reserved

By payment of the required fees, you have been granted the non-exclusive, non-transferable right to access and read the text of this book. No part of this text may be reproduced, printed, transmitted, downloaded, decompiled, reverse engineered, or stored in or introduced into any information storage and retrieval system, in any form or by any means, whether electronic or mechanical, now known or hereinafter invented, without the express written permission of the author.

Unless otherwise stated, Scripture quotations have been taken from the ESV ® Bible (The Holy Bible, English Standard Version ®), copyright © 2001 by Crossway Bible, a publishing ministry of Good News Publishers. Used by permission. All rights reserved.

Any internet addresses (websites, blogs, etc.) referenced in this book are offered as resources. They are not intended in any way to be or imply an endorsement by the author for any purpose other than that which is listed in this writing.

"What you have heard from me
in the presence of many witnesses
entrust to faithful men
who will be able to teach others also."
2 Timothy 2:2 (ESV)

THANKS

I am very grateful for the many friends and mentors who have spoken the Lord's truth into my life. While this isn't an exhaustive list, it represents those who have contributed to this writing. Thanks for the time you've spent answering my questions, wrestling over the deeper spiritual truths along with me, and diving into the deep waters of Christ's love along with me.

Jeff Miller
Dan Scarrow
Todd Sovine
Cindy and Kip Kopsick
Carol Griffith
Ami Snyder
Esteban Vazquez
Allan Riley
David Wheatley
Kurt Johnson
Bob Harner

Clint Bieri
Andy Beorn
Charlie Collier
Kurt Huber
Michael MacAdam
Jeremy Muncy
Jason Nelson
Zach Reeves
Cory Schnuerer
Andy Smith
Andy Ward

Special thanks to my wife, Sandra, for the many hours she spends listening to all of my ideas, helping me cull the good ones and toss away the bad ones, and pouring over my writings to improve them. My writing wouldn't be as effective without you.

TABLE OF CONTENTS

INTRODUCTION

**"All authority in heaven and on earth has been given to me.
Go therefore and make disciples of all nations,
baptizing them in the name of the Father and of the Son and of the Holy Spirit, teaching them to observe all that I have commanded you.
And behold, I am with you always, to the end of the age."**

-Jesus in Matthew 28:18-20.

Building Computers

Recently my youngest son built his first desktop computer. He's homeschooled, so we designed a school project out of his desire to build a computer that would allow him to excel at his gaming passion. In order to complete his "desktop computer building" class he had to answer questions like:

- What specifications are required in order to play the games that he wants to play on his new computer?
- What will the computer look like?
- What components are required to make a computer that will play the games he wants to play?
- Where are the best places to buy those components?
- What process is required to assemble the computer?
- What kind of space will the assembling process require?
- What kind of preparation does that space require to safely assemble his computer?
- How many people are required to help him in the process?
- What expertise do those people require to properly assemble the computer?
- Where do they gain that expertise?
- If he wanted to do this as a home business, at what price does he need to sell the assembled computers in order to make a profit?

See the progression of the steps? Which one of them is the most important? All of them are equally important. Which one of them isn't required? All of them are required. Take any of them out of the process and he's going to compromise the success of the project (and his grade)!

Once he's designed the computer, figured out the components required, shopped for the best place to purchase those components, researched the process to build the computer, obtained the space, fitted it for the job, assessed the amount of help required, determined the expertise those helping need to possess, developed a plan to train those helping, coach his helpers through the process, and oversee the entire operation – THEN he can begin to actually build this amazing new computer.

As he looks to see if he's able to make money off of this venture, he has to ask the question: "Is the system scalable?" It's one thing to make ***one new amazing desktop computer a day***. It's another thing to make ***a hundred new amazing desktop computers a day***. It's even another thing to make ***a thousand new amazing desktop***

computers a day. He will need more components, different space, and more employees as his plan to make more computers increases. This will require him to return to his original questions and answer them with a different goal in mind.

When he has finished building the first computer he then has to ask questions such as:

- How well does his new computer work?
- Does it play the games as well as he expected?
- What additional components would he add if he were doing it again?
- What components seem to be unnecessary?
- Would other people buy them – or is there a market for them?
- At what price does he need to sell them to make it profitable for him?

If he wants to do a good job building his computer, as well as getting a good grade in his class – and potentially making some money off of this project – he must be very intentional in what he does, how he does it, and he must take good notes throughout the process. He can't just hope to build a great computer without putting in the research. He can't hope to fit the project within his budget without doing some comparative shopping. He can't expect to get a good grade in his class without taking good notes throughout the process and writing a good report paper. He can't just hope that the components that he purchases will "fit together," hope that the computer works when he's done with it, or expect others to want to purchase one like it regardless of cost. He can't expect that mom's going to give him an A on his class just because he excels at playing games on his new computer.

Once he's successfully assembled his first desktop computer, finds that it exceeds his expectations, learns that others would be willing to pay good money for a computer just like his, and develops a process whereby he can build and sell more computers, he can't just kick his heels up on his desk and coast for the rest of his life, right? Well, I guess that he could if he was satisfied with gaining limited results, attaining only one accomplishment in his lifetime, or planned on working hard only until he could achieve a life of ease – but this wouldn't be right if he had personal integrity, if he wanted to make his mom proud, or if he wanted to build upon one success so that he could achieve even more success.

Making Disciples of Jesus Christ

This book isn't about building computers! Ha. No, it's about making disciples of Jesus Christ. Yet, there are many parallels between intentionally building computers and intentionally making disciples of Jesus Christ! The owner of the church (Jesus Christ) has tasked its members (you and I) with the job of making disciples.

Let's say that you're a pastor, an elder, or a ministry leader in the church you attend. Your job is to make disciples of Jesus Christ. If you want to be good at your disciple-making job, and please the owner of the church (Jesus Christ), you have to find the answers to questions like:

- What does a disciple of Jesus Christ look like?
- What spiritual disciplines are required for someone to develop into a fully-mature disciple of Jesus Christ?
- What personal priorities are required to develop those spiritual disciplines?
- What process is required to make disciples?
- What amount of space do we need to follow our process?
- How will that space be used?
- How many leaders are required to make disciples?
- What expertise do those leaders require to make disciples?
- Who is going to do the training?
- What financial needs are required to make disciples of Jesus Christ?

See the progression of those steps? Which one of them is the most important? All of them are equally important. Which one of them isn't required? All of them are required. Take any of them out of the process and you're going to compromise the success of the project!

Once you've determined what a disciple of Jesus Christ looks like, figured out the spiritual disciplines required to make them, ascertained the personal priorities required to develop those spiritual disciplines, developed the process, obtained the space, fitted it for the job, assessed the amount of help required, determined the expertise the leaders need to possess, developed a plan to train the leaders, coach the leaders, and manage the progress – THEN we can begin to actually make disciples of Jesus Christ.

Next you have to ask the question "Is the system scalable?" It's one thing to make ***one*** disciple of Jesus Christ a year. It's another thing to make ***a hundred*** disciples of Jesus Christ a year. It's yet another thing to make ***a thousand*** disciples of Jesus Christ a year. You will need more resources, different space, and more employees as your plan to make more disciples increases. This will require you to return to your original questions and answer them with a different goal in mind.

After you begin to actually make disciples of Jesus Christ you have to ask questions such as:

- Is our disciple-making process working to build Christ's Kingdom?
- Are those being discipled inviting others to become part of the Kingdom of Christ?
- Are those new people responding to the invitation?
- Are they becoming active parts of the church?
- What financial barriers do we have to making even more disciples?

If you want to do a good job of making disciples of Jesus Christ you must be very intentional in what you do and how you do it. You can't just show up to church without a plan and hope to make amazing disciples of Jesus Christ. You can't just hope that the disciples you're making are going to engage in spiritual disciplines on their own, that people will continue to show up on Sundays just because they found out that you're in charge of the ministry, or that the owner of the factory is going to be happy regardless of the job you're doing.

Once you've been successful at making one disciple; someone who lives their life in a way that Christ intended, who engages in spiritual disciplines, is part of the church, and you see that your process is scalable, or applicable to other areas of the church, you can't just kick your heels up on your desk and coast for the rest of your life, right? Well, I guess that would be right if you were satisfied with gaining limited results, attaining only one discipleship accomplishment in your lifetime, or planned on working hard only until you could achieve a life of ease – but this wouldn't be right if you had personal integrity, truly intended to please the owner of the church (Jesus Christ), or you wanted to build upon one success for the Kingdom so that you could achieve even more successes for the Kingdom.

All Christians Are Supposed to Make Disciples

While the above illustration is useful to get this conversation started, the points of application can be limited! It's not ***JUST*** the job of the pastor, the elder, and the ministry leader to make disciples of Jesus Christ! Making disciples of Jesus Christ is a core responsibility of each and every disciple of Jesus Christ!

In Matthew 28 we read of Christ's last words to His disciples before He returned to the Father in heaven. I think that the last words we speak at the end of our time with someone, or at the end of our life, are important words – ***very important words***. As we speak our last words we convey the most important things from our life that we wish to convey to our audience; important words that we want them to remember for the rest of their lives. As I think of the hundreds of conversations that the disciples had with Christ during their time with

Him I think there must have been hundreds of things that Jesus could have said to them as He left them to carry on the work of building His Kingdom. I think that His last words to the disciples are very important words for us to focus on today as well.

> "All authority in heaven and on earth has been given to me. Go therefore and make disciples of all nations, baptizing them in the name of the Father and of the Son and of the Holy Spirit, teaching them to observe all that I have commanded you. And behold, I am with you always, to the end of the age." Jesus in Matthew 28:18-20.

In a YouTube video entitled, *Don't be Deceived – Disciples Make Disciples*, Francis Chan and David Platt discuss some of the dynamics of being a disciple of Jesus Christ. One of their primary points is that a key mark of a disciple of Jesus Christ is that they are making other disciples of Jesus Christ. In other words: a sign that you have a genuine faith in Christ is that your faith in Christ has been replicated in the life of someone else because of the time you've spent with them. This doesn't happen by itself! It must be done very intentionally!

Conversely, we could say that if someone is not actively making disciples of Jesus Christ than we should question the barriers that are keeping them from making disciples. Perhaps they are not a true disciple themselves. They might not even be a Christian. If they have not experienced the kind of a life change that compels them to share that life change with others, and invites them to experience that same kind of a transformation in their own lives, then perhaps they haven't really met Jesus at all.

This makes sense when you think of the progression we go through in our spiritual formation. Think of someone who doesn't know Christ. They're wandering through their life without Him. They're seeking hope, deeper purpose, and the peace that passes all understanding, but they haven't found it in anything they've experienced in their lives. Then, someone brings them the good news of the Gospel Message, they find Christ, their life is transformed, and they begin to grow as His disciple. This generates a desire for them to bring this Good News to others who don't know Him. These others then find Him, begin to grow as a disciple, and share that Good News with others.

This process should develop a never-ending cycle of spiritual growth leading to evangelism that leads to discipleship that leads to more spiritual growth that leads to more evangelism that leads to more discipleship that leads to more spiritual growth – etc. etc. etc.

However, much of the time there is some kind of a disconnect in this cycle. Many of those who are professing Christians are not regularly sharing their faith with the people God has placed in their lives. They are not praying for the lost around them. They are not inviting them to church. They are not intentionally discipling those who are already in the Kingdom. They might be regular church attenders, occasional Bible readers, and even pray every once in a while. They're probably not seeing a concerted path of spiritual formation taking place in their life, can't quantify a maturing of spiritual disciplines in their life, or aren't noticing a significant life change as they follow this pattern of limited discipleship.

There is obviously a disconnection somewhere between building our own discipleship and reaching back to reach the lost and build into their discipleship. Let me posit a few thoughts on this disconnect.

1. Some would argue that those who are not actively making disciples are not part of the faith. After all, you're not a Christian just because you attend church, read your Bible, or even call yourself a Christian. Nowhere in the Bible does it say that you become a Christian when you go to the altar, raise your hand in response to an invitation, or pray a prayer for salvation. Each of these ***can be*** part of a person's spiritual journey, but they should not be the end of the journey. Perhaps some of those who have done those things have done them ***instead of*** really meeting Jesus Christ.

2. Some would argue that our modern church model only allows the "super Christians" to become the disciple-makers. We give the microphone to those who have public speaking skills, those who can learn quickly, or those who are more outgoing and we are happy to let them use their skills to teach us while telling everyone else they only need to listen and follow along in their own Bibles. Perhaps we have slowed down the spiritual formation of the individual to the speed of the class as a whole.

3. Some would say that their personal involvement at church would constitute the entirety of their personal efforts to make disciples. Maybe they teach a Sunday school class, hand out bulletins, or clean up after everyone. This is the part they play. This is the role they feel comfortable with. And, after all Paul did talk about the Body of Christ having many parts, and he said that no part is more or less important than another, right? They let those who have the microphone "lead others to Christ" and they'll just do the behind the scenes part that they're "led to do."

4. Some would argue that the focus on church programs and committees have replaced the need to be personally involved in disciple-making. We have a missions program – giving to missions is how we make disciples. We have an evangelism committee – serving on the committee, planning the events where we watch a video or listen to someone else share the Gospel Message, and inviting others to be part of the events is how we do our evangelism. Much of disciple-making is then relegated to the pastor, the elders, the church staff, and the ministry leaders. After all, that's what we're paying them for, right?

5. Some argue that there is a difference between a "Christian" and a "Disciple of Jesus Christ." They define a Christian as someone who prays to accept Christ into their life but then does little to build upon their faith. They define a disciple as someone who accepts Christ into their life and then grows in

their faith to the point where they can become a pastor or a missionary, an elder, or a ministry leader. A Christian will go to heaven when they die, but they will receive little reward for their life here on earth. Following this line of thought, a disciple is one who is daily investing in Christ's Kingdom here on earth and will be greatly rewarded when they see Him face to face.

Can We Figure It Out?

Rather than argue over potential causes for this kind of a disconnect, or debate whether or not someone is part of the Kingdom of Christ based on a prayer they once prayed, or even their church involvement, I think that our time is much better spent focusing on how we can intentionally live our lives to become mature disciples of Jesus Christ who are making more mature disciples of Jesus Christ.

That's what this book is all about. It outlines how to be a fully-devoted, mature disciple of Christ and how to make more fully-devoted, mature disciples of Jesus Christ. It includes a proven plan to meet together in intentional one-on-one discipleship relationships, as well as in small groups, to help one another become fully-devoted, mature disciples of Jesus who are actively making more fully-devoted, mature disciples of Jesus Christ.

My prayer is that the Holy Spirit uses this book to help you find at least one person who ***can disciple you*** through a one-on-one discipleship relationship and at least one person who ***you can disciple*** through a one-on-one discipleship relationship – all of us striving for the goal of becoming fully-devoted, mature disciples of Jesus Christ together.

In the Power of His Blood,

PJ Bogoniewski

Study Questions
Introduction

1. Have you ever made something from scratch? What did you make and how well did you do with the finished product?

2. When you made something, did you follow a list of instructions? Was this an easy thing to do? Why or why not?

3. When you finished your project, did you assess how well you did? What was your process? How did you score with the assessment?

4. Have you ever thought about a process to develop disciples of Jesus Christ? If you have, what kind of a process have you outlined?

5. Have you implemented your process? How well do you think you're doing? What changes do you think you have to make in order to improve your process?

6. Did you watch the YouTube video entitled, *Don't be Deceived – Disciples Make Disciples* by Francis Chan and David Platt? What was your reaction? Any thoughts to share?

7. How do you see the hand-in-hand relationship that disciple-making and evangelism hold? Explain how it should work.

8. Which of the five proposed options for the disconnect in discipleship do you resonate best with? Why?

CHAPTER 1

WHAT DOES A DISCIPLE LOOK LIKE?

**"I appeal to you therefore, brothers, by the mercies of God,
to present your bodies as a living sacrifice,
holy and acceptable to God, which is your spiritual worship.
Do not be conformed to this world,
but be transformed by the renewal of your mind,
that by testing you may discern what is the will of God,
what is good and acceptable and perfect." Romans 12:1-2.**

The term "disciple" has been used to describe a follower of Jesus Christ ever since Jesus gathered together a group of twelve guys for an intensive three year training program who then would be used by the Holy Spirit to change the world. Two-thousand years later Christian churches and leaders disagree on definitions, purposes, and practices of discipleship. While most agree that a disciple is "a follower of Jesus Christ," there is great disagreement on further definitions of what constitutes a disciple of Jesus Christ and the best process to develop true discipleship in those who are seeking it.

Convert vs Disciple

Jesus told us to do more than just make converts to Christianity – He told us to make disciples. Many of us make an effort to convert someone to Christianity, but what are we doing to make disciples? In my experience, I've noticed that there is a marked difference between converts and disciples.

Dictionary.com defines a convert as:

> To cause to adopt a different religion, political doctrine, or opinion, etc.

This is someone who has chosen to abandon their previous religious thought and replace it with another religious thought. They might transition from one kind of a church to another. They might pray a prayer or go forward at an event because they like the promise of going to heaven when they die. They may have been moved by an emotional presentation, agree to make a decision to appease a friend, or lie to someone so that they will leave them alone.

Earlier in my life I've been part of churches who engaged in street evangelism. We would meet strangers on a street corner or would go door to door to ask them some spiritual questions, try to go through the Romans Road with them, and then ask them if they'd like to pray to receive Christ. While every once in a while someone would "pray the sinners prayer," not a single person ever responded to the invitation to come to church so they could grow in their faith. For the most part people didn't want to talk with us, closed the door when we told them who we were, the church we represented, and what our purpose for our conversation was. Perhaps you've had a similar experience.

As a youth pastor I took dozens of students to evangelistic events. I saw many of them "go forward" to ask Jesus into their lives so they could go to heaven when they died, but saw few of them come to youth group on Sunday so they could grow in their "newfound faith."

Are these people truly saved? Have they experienced a life change? Will they truly be in heaven forever when they die or have we just given them a false view of what being a believer in Jesus Christ is really all about? Will they spend an eternity separated from God saying something like, "But PJ told me I was going to heaven when I died if I said this prayer..."

Now, you have to hear me clearly on this. I don't have any problem with either of these plans, as well as dozens of similar evangelism methods as long as they are part of an intentional plan to make disciples rather than make converts. Our goal is not to get someone to pray a prayer, change their religious viewpoints, or get them to attend our church. Our goal has to be to introduce them to Jesus Christ and let Him transform their lives through the power of His Holy Spirit. In my experience, someone who has experienced the life transformation that comes through true relationship with Jesus Christ ***wants*** to be in church, ***wants*** to grow in their faith, and is ***excited*** about being part of a discipleship process. Yet in my life, I've seen that there are many who profess to be a Christian who are not interested in any of these things. This cases me to question the validity of their faith.

A rounded definition of a disciple shows us that it's a far deeper commitment than that of a convert. A disciple of Jesus Christ is a ***student of Jesus Christ***, who is submitting themselves to be daily transformed into the image of Jesus Christ. I've found that the best way to develop disciples of Jesus Christ is through the experience of relationship, through the development of biblical knowledge, and through effective service as part of the body of Christ.

The experience of relationship includes their relationship with Jesus Christ, their relationship with someone who is actively involved in discipling them, their relationship with the Body of Christ, and their relationships with the lost people around them. Disciples must develop biblical knowledge and learn how to apply that knowledge to their lives. We must also be involved in works of service for the Body of Christ, His church.

In Ephesians 2 Paul tells us that we were created for works of service:

> "For by grace you have been saved through faith. And this is not your own doing; it is the gift of God, not a result of works, so that no one may boast. For we are his workmanship, created in Christ Jesus for good works, which God prepared beforehand, that we should walk in them." Ephesians 2:8-10.

I'm not sure where some people got the idea that they were saved just so they could get to heaven one day. While heaven is a great and glorious promise for the believer, Paul affirms that we have so much more to experience while we are here on this earth – and that we experience much of that as we fellowship with and serve others.

Ultimately, the development of our own discipleship leads us to share our faith with others and this develops the need for them to be discipled as well. They grow in their faith, reach out to others, and then have to disciple them. True discipleship is a never-ending circle of spiritual growth, personal evangelistic outreach, and then more discipling.

Intentional Discipleship

Defining the attributes required in a disciple of Jesus Christ and developing a process to transform lost people into mature disciples of Jesus Christ should be a crucial step in the development and implementation of the spiritual formation plan in every church or ministry. I embrace the definition that Paul gives us for a mature believer in Ephesians 4, and I believe every church leader must seriously consider the role he or she is playing in developing maturity in those Christ has put under their care:

> "To equip the saints for the work of ministry, for building up the body of Christ, until we all attain to the unity of the faith and of the knowledge of the Son of God, to mature manhood, to the measure of the stature of the fullness of Christ, so that we may no longer be children, tossed to and fro by the waves and carried about by every wind of doctrine, by human cunning, by craftiness in deceitful schemes. Rather, speaking the truth in love, we are to grow up in every way into him who is the head, into Christ, from whom the whole body, joined and held together by every joint with which it is equipped, when each part is working properly, makes the body grow so that it builds itself up in love." Ephesians 4:12-16.

Based on Paul's perspective, I've developed the following working definition of a disciple of Jesus Christ:

> A disciple is ***a student of Jesus Christ***, who is submitting themselves to be transformed into the image of Jesus Christ, through the experience of relationship, through the development of biblical knowledge, and through effective service as part of the body of Christ.

This definition was developed through the teachings of 1 Corinthians 12, Romans 12, Ephesians 2, Ephesians 4, Romans 8, James 2, and many other Scripture passages.

Let's look at each of the components of this definition point by point.

Transformed Into the Image of Christ

We have to remember that our goal is help transform people into the image of Jesus Christ. This can only be done by Jesus as He accomplishes His work through the power of His Holy Spirit. Our objective is not to get people to think the way we think, be skilled in the areas that we're skilled, or follow the path we've designed for them. Rather than play the part of the Holy Spirit in their lives, I want to help them hear the voice of God speaking to them through the Holy Spirit. There is a marked difference between helping someone ***hear from God*** and being the person who ***speaks for God***. One helps someone hear the voice of God speaking in their life and lets God speak for Himself. The other assumes that we know what God would say in various situations and gives guidance based on what we think He would say or do. One leads to significant life change. The other leads to life change that is minimal at best. I'd rather let God speak for Himself and help others hear what He is saying to them and watch Him do His amazing work of life change.

To do this we must see our role as that of helping them understand what they're reading in Scripture, helping them to hear the voice of the Lord speaking in their life, teaching them how to apply what they're reading and hearing from Him, and helping them be involved in acts of service for the Kingdom. I view my role in discipleship as a guide or a mentor, not as an authority in their lives, or someone who simply tells them everything I think they need to do.

Development of Biblical Knowledge

I embrace the argument that you must have a working understanding of Scripture in order to live a life of discipleship that pleases Christ. You simply cannot go through life defining your own definition of sin, your own definition of holy living, or hoping that you'll just intuitively know what Christ would have you do, guessing how Jesus thinks or feels about certain situations you encounter, and hoping that He's pleased with the choices you make. Jesus is the only one who defines what it means to be a Christian. We learn that definition as we study Scripture and apply its truths to our lives. A disciple has to be devoted to deeper Bible study with the intention of following the Holy Spirit's lesson of application for our daily lives.

Jesus clearly defined His expectations for His disciples. The Gospels are full of Christ's commands for us, His admonitions for us, and His expectations for us – as well as the stories of those who either accepted or rejected those commands, admonitions, and expectations. I don't think that these discipleship parameters are any different for us 2,000 years later. Many of these commands, admonitions, and expectations are very, very difficult to accept. If we think that we can pick and choose which we can follow and which we can ignore then we are simply defining our own religion and we most certainly are not a true disciple of Jesus Christ.

We must surrender our lives to Christ every day and allow Him to be the one who determines what it really means to follow Him! Consider the following passages where Christ told of His expectations for His disciples:

- "If anyone does not abide in me he is thrown away like a branch and withers; and the branches are gathered, thrown into the fire, and burned." John 15:6.
- "If you love me, you will keep my commandments." John 14:15.
- "Whoever does not love me does not keep my words." John 14:24.
- "Whoever is of God hears the words of God. The reason why you do not hear them is that you are not of God." John 8:47.
- "If anyone comes to me and does not hate his own father and mother and wife and children and brothers and sisters, yes, and even his own life, he cannot be my disciple." Luke 14:26.
- "Salt is good, but if salt has lost its taste, how shall its saltiness be restored? It is of no use either for the soil or for the manure pile. It is thrown away." Luke 14:34-35.
- "For if you forgive others their trespasses, your heavenly Father will also forgive you, but if you do not forgive others their trespasses, neither will your Father forgive your trespasses." Matthew 6:14-15.
- So Jesus said to the Jews who had believed him, "If you abide in my word, you are truly my disciples." John 8:31
- Then Jesus told his disciples, "If anyone would come after me, let him deny himself and take up his cross and follow me. For

> whoever would save his life will lose it, but whoever loses his life for my sake will find it." Matthew 16:24-25.

Scripture doesn't specifically cover the how-to's for every area of our lives, but it does clearly convey concepts that will allow us to make wise decisions regarding every area of our modern culture. A disciple of Jesus Christ is only going to learn these things by dedicating themselves to becoming a diligent student of God's Written Word. I have taught basic exegetical and hermeneutical concepts and practices through sermons, Sunday school classes, small group discussions, pieces of writing, conversations on Facebook, and in one-on-one discipleship meetings. I have taught these things to Jr. High students, Sr. High students, college students, and to adults of all ages. I have also covered these topics in leadership training times, on retreats, and at Christian camps. I believe they are crucial skills for every disciple of Jesus Christ to know and employ. I do not embrace the idea that says that only Bible teachers need to know and implement these things. I believe that every disciple of Jesus Christ should understand and implement them as they engage in their daily Bible study.

If you have not developed at least basic exegetical or hermeneutical skills, or if those terms are foreign to you, I highly recommend you read the book, *How to Read The Bible For All It's Worth*, by Stuart and Fee. Rather than summarize these processes here, I point you to their book in order to gain a working understanding of how to properly read the Bible and apply its principles into your life. I also cover this question in my book, *Got Questions? Jesus Has the Answers! Volume I.*

Through the Experience of Relationship

Any discipleship focus cannot be solely based on learning the Bible. As I meet with others to disciple them I focus on developing our relationship together, becoming friends with them for discipleship purposes, as well as helping them further develop their relationship with Christ. Yes, I care about the biblical head knowledge that someone I'm discipling is developing, as well as knowing how to apply it to their lives, but I care more about the heart-felt love that they have for Jesus, and how that love for Him spills over into the lives of others around them. As I devote myself to helping them develop a closer, more personal relationship with Christ, I know that relationship will spill over into the lives of others through acts of service.

Effective Service as Part of the Body of Christ

It is not possible to be a disciple of Jesus Christ without serving Him by serving others. In 1 Corinthians 12 and Romans 12 Paul teaches those respective churches that God has gifted His people so that they will serve each other and complete His mission. He is the one who chooses the gifts, the amount of time we experience those gifts, and the mission for the church. There is room and opportunity within the Body of Christ for every disciple of Jesus Christ to serve Him by serving others ***SOMEHOW***! Not everyone is going to become a pastor or missionary, an elder, a board member, or a ministry leader; but everyone can find a way to serve the Body of Christ – and to serve those who are yet to be part of the Body of Christ. We can use our talents, our interests, our abilities, as well as depend on the spiritual gifts that Jesus promised to provide through His Holy Spirit as we are daily following Him.

It's usually easy for us to see how pastors, missionaries, elders, deacons, deaconesses, and ministry leaders serve the church. There are others who are serving the Body of Christ in ways that we may never see. They are just as important as those who are serving in visible ways!

I know a guy who will never be chosen to lead worship on a Sunday morning, never be asked to present the sermon, do announcements, teach a Sunday school class, or lead a small group. He'll probably never be asked to be a ministry leader, serve on a board, or stand on the platform on a Sunday morning, but he serves Jesus Christ each and every day – and He ministers to the Body of Christ and those who are not part of the Body of Christ each day. He lives in a state where there is a deposit on soda and beer cans. He collects them from people at church, friends, neighbors, as well as picking them up on the side of the road, in public trash cans – wherever he can find them. He cashes in the money and gives it to missionary work. Rather than use this money to buy stuff for himself, he uses this money to expand the Kingdom in far-away places. You would probably never know what he's doing with all the cans he collects. You might even question or mock him if you saw him walking by the side of the road to pick up cans, or go through public garbage containers to find more "money" he can invest in the Kingdom. You're never going to hear him brag about what he's doing, but his work is being noted by the King of Kings, and there will be a day where he will be rewarded for all that he's done to advance the Kingdom!

I also know of a woman whose ministry to the church was to prepare the flowers for the altar on Sunday mornings. She not only made the arrangements herself, but she grew the flowers in her own garden specifically for the purpose of cutting them, arranging them, and placing them on the altar each Sunday morning. She put care and concern into the flowers from even before she planted the seeds. As she cultivated her garden she prayed over those who would be hearing the Word of God preached as they looked upon the flowers she put there. During the cold weather she either solicited donations from local nurseries or spent her own money to purchase the flowers she used that Sunday. She too never preached or taught, but she used her green thumb to honor Jesus and to bless those who attended that church. Only the pastor knew she was the one who provided the flowers every week. In fact, the rest of the church found out about her ministry during the announcement of her funeral, where she requested that flowers not be given for her funeral, but that money is given to the church to allow her to provide for flowers on the altar long after her passing.

Churches need pastors, elders, board members, Sunday school teachers, worship leaders, ministry leaders, custodians, secretaries, people to help watch kids in the nursery, someone to cut the grass, people to organize and cook for the pot luck suppers, and a myriad of other people to do an endless list of other things – but they also need people to use their everyday talents and abilities, their habits and hobbies, their time and resources to invest in the Kingdom of God outside of the church walls.

Just think of what Christ's Kingdom would look like if every disciple of Jesus Christ would embrace the idea that their service to others was part of their service to the King and desired to impact the lives of others for the Kingdom ***somehow*** every single day!

Being a Student of Christ

Consider the following aspects implied in the term "student:"

- A student learns from a teacher.
- A student follows a course of learning.
- A student has to complete homework.
- A student is given projects to work on.
- A student takes notes.
- A student studies outside of the classroom to further their learning.
- A student is tested and graded.
- A student moves on once they have passed the test.

I realize that using the term "student" may bring a variety of different word pictures into your mind. Some of them may be good – some of them may be bad. Most of them may involve your childhood and teenage years. Some of them involve college study. You may have been a good student or perhaps you've struggled with learning for most of your life. You might have embraced your college education or kept away from careers that required further study. You may have done very well in college, squeaked by, or dropped out.

You may have carried these thoughts on being a student into your relationship with Jesus. I assume that if your educational experiences did not end well then you do not look at your relationship with Christ as one that would require the components of being a student listed above. You probably look at your relationship with Christ on par with most of the relationships that you have in your life. When most of us spend time with our friends, we do things like enjoying music together, watching TV and movies together, we catch a sporting event together, or we hang out playing pool, ping-pong, or board games together – but we don't really expect to learn much from our friends while we spend time together.

I see this perspective in many who attend church on Sunday mornings. They're there to spend time with Jesus, they enjoy the music, they appreciate the sermon, and they leave with little to no intention of doing much with what they ***learned*** through the experience. They'll be back in a week or two, and they really appreciate the events that serve food, but they're not attending to learn, to be stretched, or to find out how to amend their day-to-day lives.

Once a student who desires to learn has completed a formal educational program they continue to read non-fiction books to learn, to study, or to expand their knowledge in an area that they have a personally invested interest. Nobody tells them what they should continue to read on their own. Nobody assigns them homework. They continue to utilize their study skills on their own, or they seek out someone who can help them take their knowledge to the next level.

There are also those who end their education and say, "Now that I'm done with that I'm not reading another book ever again!" They don't look to learn, to study, or expand their knowledge in any area of their lives. They will probably gain more knowledge through their day to day interaction with others, and as they go about their job, but it will probably happen in a haphazard manner, and it will take much longer than it would if they were following an intentional approach.

The statistics show that about half of us are comfortable never reading another book on our own to learn something for the rest of our lives. According to a HuffPost/YouGov poll that asked 1,000 US adults about their reading habits, they found that 42 percent had not read a nonfiction book in the past year (HuffPost). Other things that I've read indicate that the trend is leading towards people reading ***LESS*** non-fiction the further they get from completing their high school or college education.

This reminds me of a sad story that John Piper tells in his book, *Don't Waste Your Life* of a couple who were looking forward to achieving early retirement so that they could spend the rest of their lives walking on the seashore collecting shells and playing softball. They were content by doing very little with this era of their lives even though they had great potential of mentoring others. They had no plans to achieve, to learn, to grow, or to accomplish anything of value once they reached "the end of their working lives." Yet my reading of Scripture tells me that we were made for so much more than something like this!

Our relationship with Christ should be so much more than "hanging out with Jesus" when we attend church! We should be seeing Him change us into His image as we regularly read His Written Word, hear His voice in listening prayer, allow the Holy Spirit to move in our hearts to apply what we read, and willingly embrace the changes He has ahead for us. So many of us just want to live a comfortable life with Jesus by our side, but Jesus wants us to get out of our comfort zone and experience all that He has planned for us. This requires us to see ourselves as students of Scripture and full participants in His Kingdom work. To be a true disciple of Jesus Christ we must read, we must study, we must follow His leading, we must be tested – and we must carry this perspective with us for the rest of our lives.

Learning Techniques

Talk to any professional teacher and you'll hear that a good teacher employs a variety of learning techniques to educate their students. Some of them are more intellectual, some are more hands on; some require extra time of personal study, and others need to be developed with the needs of individual students in mind. Just as a good school teacher uses creative means to convey the three R's of a good education to their students, a good discipleship mentor is going to employ a variety of learning techniques in order to teach their students to be a disciple of Christ.

Think of the differences in each of these learning dynamics:

- A lecture hall in a large college.
- A one room schoolhouse.
- A classroom in a poverty-stricken area.
- Reading a book while lying on a hammock.
- A classroom that is fully-fitted with electronics.
- A homeschooling parent.
- A shop apprentice.
- A young adult attending night school.
- Taking classes through a correspondence school.
- Going through a book study with accompanying video in a small group.
- Sitting with someone on-on-one to answer their specific questions on a topic.

Can you picture the student sitting in the lecture hall with her book and notes open on her desk? Can you picture the guy up to his arms in the engine compartment while his teacher talks him through the steps required to change the alternator? Can you picture an older student teaching a younger one to read in the one room schoolhouse? (Depending on how old you are, I bet you can't do this without thinking about *Little House on the Prairie.*) Can you picture the girl sending an email to her teacher who is on the video screen in a tech-savvy classroom? Can you picture the young man trying to keep his eyes open at night school – tired from the full day shift he worked so that he could earn enough to finish his education? Can you picture the woman pouring over the Beth Moore study notes as she listens to the video presentation with her small group? Can you see the young man laying brick on the wall – his hands being guided by the expert mason? Can you see the couple sitting to talk at the coffee shop, leaning towards each other to engage in a personal conversation?

All of these can be effective learning dynamics for the Kingdom as well!

For the most part, the learning model that most modern churches have adapted is a "one-to-many" learning environment. We can compare it to the college venue of a large lecture hall that is mostly communicating head knowledge to its students. We've developed a "come and listen" model that is designed to take 20-30 years to transform a non-believer into a disciple of Jesus Christ. This is not a good design to meet everyone where they are in their faith and help them take the next steps on their faith journey. Study after study shows that it isn't a model that allows for a quick learning plan and isn't doing a good enough job of developing maturity of faith and effective servants for Christ's Kingdom.

As a homeschool dad I've learned that there are three primary ways students learn: by hearing, by seeing, or by experiencing. Some students need to see something with their eyes to get it. They have to write it down, they have to read it somewhere, and they have to see a video, or see a demonstration of something. Others are auditory learners. They have to hear someone explain it to them. Others are hands-on learners. They have to tinker with things to figure them out for themselves.

A teacher is going to find students with multiple learning styles within any classroom setting. If a teacher wants to communicate to all of their students then they must employ a variety of means to communicate their lessons. They must find ways to communicate to the visual learner, the auditory learner, and the hands-on learner. This is one reason why I use visual overheads (such as Power Point or Prezi) for my sermon and teaching notes, incorporate pictures and videos, as well as print out a version of my notes for everyone in attendance. Those who are auditory learners benefit from hearing me teach. They benefit even more if they're able to ask questions. Those who are visual can follow along with my notes on the screen, watch the videos, and read along with the notes on their lap. Those who have to experience something "hands on" can doodle on their note sheets, fill in the blanks, or engage with the videos or illustrations I provide. They also best respond to the challenges I make to "do something" to respond to the lesson. This is also why I facilitate interactive events for prayer, study, evangelism, and service. I realize that some people can best learn by doing and I have to provide a venue for them to come and ***learn by doing*** rather than having to ***learn before doing.***

A Disciple is an Apprentice

There is another aspect of the definition of a disciple that involves "doing something" with the lessons that are being learned. I also like to use the word ***apprentice*** within my definition of the word disciple. While the term "student" describes the learning aspect of our discipleship, the term "apprentice" adds the act of doing something with the learning that the student is receiving. It also implies that the teacher is incorporating "hands on lessons" with the student. A disciple of Jesus Christ isn't someone who just ***knows*** what Jesus wants them to know. A disciple is someone who then ***does*** what they are ***learning*** they should do. The "learning" and the "doing" must go hand-in-hand.

Also inherent in the term "apprentice" is the plan for the eventual replacement of the teacher by the apprentice (the teacher steps down and the apprentice takes their spot) – or seeing the apprentice begin a new work of ministry (similar to the ministry work of the teacher or a completely new work). In a discipleship setting, the person being discipled should be learning how to read and study the Bible on their own, how to share their faith on their own, as well as the personal nurture of their spiritual growth, and the development of other spiritual disciplines –and how to lead others to do the same. They may also be learning aspects of leadership that is specialized specifically for the area of ministry they are being called to lead.

Being a disciple of Jesus Christ involves more than coming to church, engaging in worship, occasionally reading your Bible, praying before meals, and trying your best to apply what you hear in the sermon on Sunday to your daily life. It involves positioning yourself in a place of deeper study, engaging in listening prayer, being part of a genuine community, and serving Christ through a healthy, vibrant church, as well as in your personal life.

We should all have the goal of being a mature disciple of Jesus Christ who is making more mature disciples of Jesus Christ. The entire New Testament encourages us to be fully-devoted, mature disciples of Jesus Christ and encourages us to allow our relationship with Christ to change us, ministering to others as a result of the work that Christ is doing in us. There is no option to just "coast through life as a Christian until we get to heaven!"

Assessment is Key

Just as assessment in a college degree is a crucial component of knowing when someone has grasped the material well enough to take the next steps, assessment of spiritual formation is a crucial step for the disciple of Christ to know where he or she is in their faith and what steps are next for them. In fact, we all need to ask questions on our spiritual journey on a regular basis: Questions like: "Where do I stand in my walk with Christ?" "Paul calls us to work towards maturity, so how mature am I?" "How can I tell?" "What are the next steps before me in my journey?"

As Paul was writing to the church in Corinth, he encourages them to go through a process of self-evaluation to see if they are in the faith:

> "Examine yourselves, to see whether you are in the faith. Test yourselves. Or do you not realize this about yourselves, that Jesus Christ is in you?—unless indeed you fail to meet the test!" 2 Corinthians 13:5.

Often we try to determine these things on our own and then find out that our matrix to ascertain our progress in our own spiritual journey is somehow flawed. We all wish to do well, but many times we find that we have set the bar much lower than it should be and we're not experiencing the results we were hoping for. We need to invite others who are more mature in their faith than we are to play a primary role in the process of defining the goal and determining how well we're hitting the mark. None of us like to hear that we're not doing as well as we think, but we cannot become a mature disciple of Christ without developing the spiritual discipline of honest assessment and correction. Christ often chided His disciples, but coupled His criticism with steps of improvement to take and a promise that He would be there with them as they took those steps. Those who refused to take those steps were left where they were as they contemplated if they were willing to surrender their lives and do things God's way. If they were, they remained part of the group. If they weren't, they no longer had the privilege of being in Christ's inner circle. It was just too uncomfortable for them to remain part of the group after they had rejected His teaching.

In Matthew 19 we read the story of a rich young man who came to Christ to ask what he needed to do to gain eternal life. Jesus told him, "Sell what you possess and give to the poor, and you will have treasure in heaven; and come, follow me." (Matthew 19:21.) Jesus was assessing where this young man was in his faith and giving him the next challenge that was required in his walk with God. Rather than accept the challenge, verse 22 says, "When the young man heard this he went away sorrowful, for he had great possessions." He chose to keep his possessions in the "top spot" of his life rather than surrender them to God and follow Jesus. Many of us do this very same thing when we fail to be assessed, or reject the assessment of our lives that Scripture so clearly provides.

Sometimes we find that we're trying to lower the bar of expectations that Jesus gives us in Scripture. Rather than amend our lives so that we can strive for His high demands, we amend Scripture so that His demands easily fit into our daily lives. Simply put: this is sin. It's not possible to follow Christ with a definition of discipleship that *we have defined for ourselves.* Jesus is the one – and He is the only one – who can define what it means to be His disciple. We must seek His definition from the pages of Scripture and submit fully to His definition of discipleship.

In John Chapter 6 we read of a time where Jesus clearly describes the bar He has set for His disciples. Many of them, seeing what He demanded of them, decided they were no longer going to follow Him.

> "After this many of his disciples turned back and no longer walked with him. So Jesus said to the Twelve, "Do you want to go away as well?" Simon Peter answered him, "Lord, to whom shall we go? You have the words of eternal life, and we have believed, and have come to know, that you are the Holy One of God." John 6:66-69.

Jesus was not afraid to set the bar where He knew it needed to be and let others decide if they were going to strive to reach it or bail out. Nowhere in Scripture do we see Jesus lowering His expectations because the majority of people thought they were too high. Nowhere in Scripture do we see Jesus changing His initial call so that someone who had rejected Him would change their minds and join the team. He set the bar high. He taught those who were willing to strive for that bar. Through His Holy Spirit He empowered them to meet those expectations. He offers this same challenge and promise to us today.

Too many times pastors and ministry leaders are pressured into lowering their bar of expectations for those serving in the church. Even though they have the training and the experience to know what should be expected of those who are leading in the church they are forced to employ dynamics that are almost always doomed to fail. Many times these same people who have demanded lowered expectations blame the pastor or ministry leader for failing to succeed under the ministry environment created by these lower expectations. We should strive to allow Jesus to define the expectations for those serving in His church and all of us; pastors, ministry leaders, and people in the pews should submit ourselves to His expectations and qualifications.

Tools for Assessment

It is helpful for us to use tools to assess both personal and ministry qualifications, expectations, and effectiveness. Dan Spader studied the model of ministry that Jesus Christ used as He ministered to others and trained His disciples to join Him in that ministry. Spader used Christ's model to develop a modern ministry model we can use to reach the lost and see them develop into mature disciples of Christ. He entitled this modern model *Growing a Healthy Church*. Ministry leaders can study and apply this model through a book by the same title, as well as interactive healthy ministry training events by the same name. Spader also developed a matrix to gauge the spiritual formation of a follower of Christ. He divided the journey of discipleship into seven steps and developed a list of specific spiritual traits that disciples of Christ can use as a benchmark to see where they are on the path to become a mature disciple. While there can be no "ONE CHART to rule them all," a tool like this becomes an indication of where our ultimate goal is, where we currently are in our journey, and what some of our next steps may be. It must be used, both personally and within a ministry, with a concerted covering of prayer and sensitivity to the work of the Holy Spirit, as well as an understanding that none of us have reached full maturity in Christ yet, but that Christ meets us where we are and empowers us to take the next steps as we humble ourselves before Him.

Here is an adaptation of Spader's matrix designed to help anyone identify where they are on the path of spiritual formation which leads to a mature disciple of Jesus Christ. As I work with those who would like to assess their discipleship progress, I ask them to check the boxes of the stages of discipleship they've achieved. Have they helped with ministries in the church? Check those boxes. Do they read their Bible, pray on a regular basis, and engage in other spiritual disciplines? Check the boxes that best represent their spiritual disciplines. Do they tithe to their local church? Do they give over and above that tithe for other ministries or needs as they're presented to them? Check those boxes. Do they share their faith, engage in spiritual conversations with their neighbors, coworkers, or family members? Check those boxes. Ultimately, our goal is to become a fully-devoted, mature disciple of Jesus Christ who is living our life in a missional way.

I've yet to find anyone who could check ALL of the boxes! I haven't checked all of the boxes in my life yet. And I'm sure as you read over this list you can easily come up with other items that could be added to the list. This list isn't exhaustive by any means, but it serves as a simple assessment tool that becomes a starting point for a conversation on the next discipleship steps ahead of us. We all have more progress to make on our journey to be completely mature in our faith!

Perhaps you want to check the boxes for yourself to see how you size up on this evaluation.

If the image on the following page is too small to see, you can find a link to a larger image at:

www.ActsofLight.com/acts/books.htm

Notice the progression from church-centered activities on the left to missional living components on the right. It's possible for someone to stay busy with church activities and never progress past the first three steps. Those who are able to progress to steps 5-7 are able to have the greatest impact on reaching others for Christ and making disciples who make more disciples. This needs to be the goal of every disciple of Jesus Christ.

Discipleship Assessment Sheet

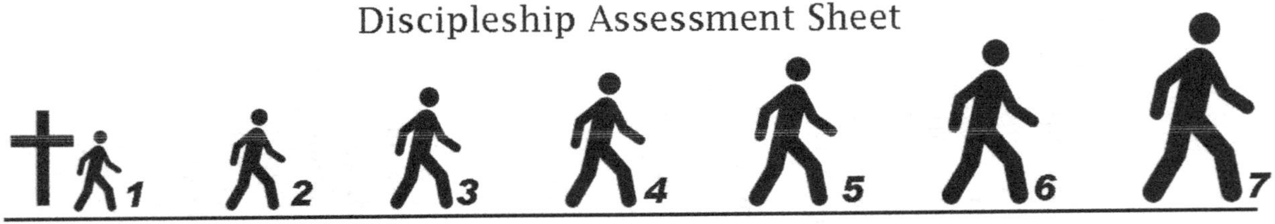

1	2	3	4	5	6	7
Service to those within the church			Inviting others into the church			Living Missionally
◊ Cleaning	◊ Teaching a Kids ministry class	◊ Teaching a Sunday school class	◊ Regularly invite people from church into your home	◊ Regularly invite non-Christians into your home	◊ Regularly talking with non-Christians about their faith	◊ Starting relationships so that you can share your faith
◊ Food prep	◊ Leadership over the toddler room	◊ Leading a small group study	◊ Praying with people at church about their needs	◊ Praying with/for non-Christians	◊ Being involved with Bible studies/small groups with non-Christians	◊ Strategizing dark areas that you can bring light to
◊ On a worship team	◊ Leading a worship team	◊ Less than a tithe support of the local church	◊ Attending the prayer sessions	◊ Meeting felt needs of non-Christians	◊ Using outreach events to invite others to find out about Christ	◊ Starting Bible studies/small groups with non-Christians
◊ Working sound board	◊ Serving on the Board	◊ Some giving to the GCF or mission trips	◊ Tithing your income to the local church	◊ Tithing your income to the local church	◊ More than tithing your income to the local church	◊ Hosting outreach events to reach others for Christ
◊ Faith in action events	◊ Attending Sunday School	◊ Have witnessed your faith to **some** co-workers or friends	◊ Serving on the Elder board	◊ More intentional giving to the GCF or short-term Missions projects	◊ Being involved in an intentional 3-way discipleship relationship (behind, level, ahead)	◊ More than tithing your income to the local church
◊ Greeting team	◊ Give to the church when you can	◊ Being involved in the planning/development of a VBS	◊ Ministry leader/staff member	◊ Daily devotional/prayer life	◊ Reading more intense discipleship material	◊ Giving a tithe to the GCF or other missions projects
◊ Making coffee	◊ Teaching a VBS class	◊ Every few days devotional/prayer life	◊ Attending vision/leadership sessions	◊ Regularly using spiritual gifts	◊ Training others to be used in ministry	◊ Writing material for others to use
◊ Project-oriented mission trips	◊ Occasional devotional/prayer life	◊ 75% or more church attendance	◊ Every other day devotional/prayer life	◊ Building into the lives of current leaders		◊ Raising leaders from the harvest
◊ Working in the toddler room	◊ 1/2 time church attendance	◊ Hearing the conviction of the Holy Spirit	◊ Identifying spiritual gifts	◊ Regularly engaging in listening prayer and following Him		
◊ Taking part in fellowship events	◊ Helping with youth ministry		◊ Responding to the conviction of the Holy Spirit			
◊ Casual giving to the church						
◊ Being involved with VBS						
◊ Hit or miss devotional/prayer life						
◊ Occasional church attendance						

Adapted from: Growing a Healthy Church Materials

WARNING: Not Everyone Wants to be Assessed

The original purpose of the adaptation of the above chart was to use it as a self-assessment tool for those who said they wanted to take intentional steps of development in their own personal spiritual formation. To some extent, the use of this chart failed miserably. I learned a few important things from the experiment of using this chart for personal assessment.

1. Many of those who scored 1-3 on this chart thought they should have tested much higher than they did. Many of them were upset with me for testing them. Some decided to attend another church shortly after taking the test. Some never spoke to me again. After seeing the results of the test, some reported they were quite comfortable not knowing how they were doing, and handed the test back to me.

2. Many of those who scored 5-7 on this chart thought they should have tested lower than they did. Many of them took on the challenge of stepping up their walk with Christ so they could make it to the next level within the next year. Many of them had checked almost everything except to initiate relationships with those around them for the purpose of sharing the Gospel message (which is missional living). Some of them took on the challenge to learn how to live their lives missionally.

3. Many people have adopted a model of spiritual maturity that is solely based on their church involvement. This means that they were given leadership responsibilities at church although they were only a 2 or 3 on the matrix. They thought they had reached spiritual maturity and couldn't believe there were 4 or 5 stages of development ahead of them. I think this is a fault of a discipleship model that only involves church attendance, or is based on a ceiling that is caused by being involved with only one specific ministry in the church.

4. There were very few people who had an understanding of the missional living steps. They thought that attaining the position of a board member or an elder were the highest things on God's scale of discipleship. Many who took the assessment thought anything above board member or elder were steps reserved for pastors and missionaries.

5. Some people rejected the concept of being assessed at church. Some said that assessment belonged in the educational system and on the job, but never at church. They thought that leadership at a church should be glad to have a person's service regardless of their aptitude, their commitment, or its spiritual fruit. Some argued that Jesus never had expectations of His disciples and the modern church shouldn't have any expectations of its people today. (I don't think this attitude can be argued biblically.)

6. The last point that I learned through this experiment is that many of the people who say they want to be assessed really don't want to be assessed. They just want to hear that they're doing a good job and are appreciated for what they're doing. When they found out that they were low on the scale, they rejected the test, or the person administrating the test.

The last two points have really gnawed at me. This is really different from the way I was raised in the church. I welcomed assessment and looked forward to the times that spiritual mentors outlined the next steps ahead of me. I was taught to strive to give my best to Christ and rejoiced at the fruit I saw the Holy Spirit doing in my life and through my life. Have we lost the concept that we're to give our best to Christ? Where did we abandon excellence for convenience? Where did we pick up the idea that a warm body in a ministry position is a good thing? Doesn't a student want to get the A+ on a paper anymore? Don't they strive for it, study for it, and rejoice when they earn it? Don't they want the teacher to think they are a good student? Aren't we working hard for the King, realizing that one day we're going to stand accountable before Him, wanting to hear Him say, "Well done, good and faithful servant?" Have we forgotten that only those who follow Christ's commandments and strive to build into His Kingdom in His ways will be the ones to hear His approval when we stand before Him face to face? Are we afraid to teach these aspects of discipleship, develop a system in which true disciples are "grown," or do we just develop a system that is based on a "comfortable norm?"

Spiritual Formation Can Be Charted

While it's not possible to develop a chart that can highlight every possible stage of a person's spiritual formation, I believe that it is possible to highlight some of the typical milestones a believer will experience in their spiritual formation that are required to become a fully-devoted, mature disciple of Jesus Christ. At a very minimum, a tool can help us ascertain if someone is making steps of forward progress, standing still, or moving backwards.

James Engel, in his book entitled *What's Gone Wrong With the Harvest,* developed a span of spiritual maturity that ranges from -8 to +8. Those on the negative side are people who have varied levels of exposure to the Gospel, but have not yet believed in Christ. A person at zero is someone who has just placed their dependence on Jesus Christ. From there, he outlined 8 levels of growth in Christ that represent the positive side of the spectrum.

Engel's Scale can be a helpful tool to see how God is working in our lives at various stages, the role you play as you disciple others to take steps of spiritual formation, as well as the stages of response on the part of the person being discipled. One of the things that I like best about Engel's Scale is that every single person on the face of the earth is ***somewhere*** on Engel's Scale. As a pastor, I can use this scale to identify where a person is in their spiritual maturity and develop a learning plan to help them take the next steps.

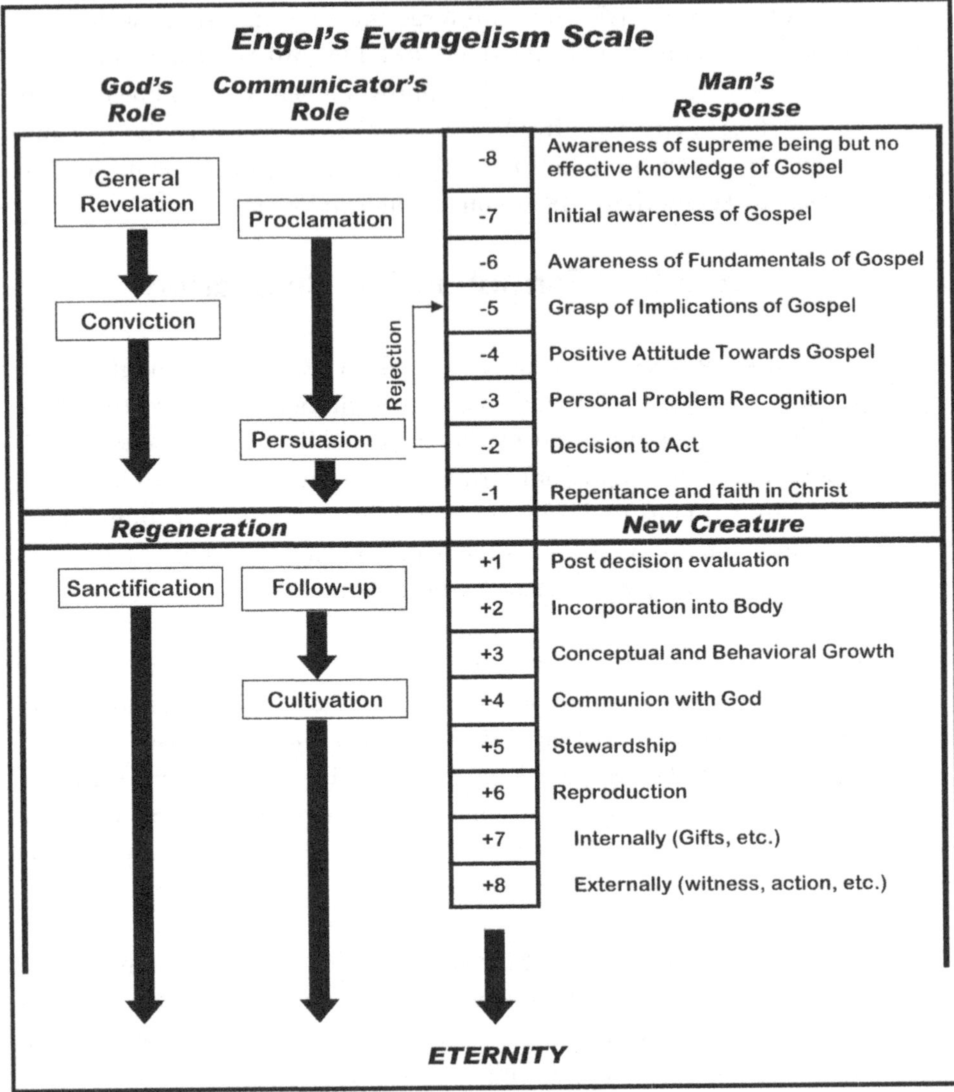

Everyone is somewhere on this chart. Look at Engel's Scale carefully. Where are you? What are your next steps? Think about others in your life. Where are they? What are their next steps? Take a moment to pray about those next steps and how you can play a role in helping them identify them and take them further on their spiritual journey.

Sadly, any one of us can stop the process of spiritual growth at any point – both on the negative side or the positive side of the point where we know Jesus. Of course, God's design is that we all grow to complete maturity in Christ. His revelation and conviction never end, and once we've given our lives to Him the process of sanctification will continue until we see Him face to face. We should be on a never-ending trajectory of being convicted of our sin, confessing our sin, repenting of our sin, and growing closer to the image of Christ. This trajectory of discipleship in our own lives leads to outreach – and outreach leads to the need for discipleship. The two work hand-in-hand.

It's Key to Develop Maturity

It's hard to define the word "maturity" in a definitive manner. If you ask people around you to define maturity you will hear them offer a wide variety of answers. If you ask them how to determine when someone has passed from immaturity to maturity most of them will say, "I don't know." The American culture doesn't have a clear way to classify a time or involve a certain event where someone moves from the position of immaturity to maturity. In some undeveloped countries, and in past cultures, most women were considered mature when they were able to have children, and boys had to face an event or a task that they had to complete to be considered a man. Some challenge their young men to jump off of this cliff with a rope tied to your ankle. If the boy has the guts to jump (and survives it) they are now an adult. Or they might have been invited on their first hunt. They went into the hunt as a child, but if they killed their first animal on a hunt they came back into the village as a man. If they were unsuccessful then they were considered to be a child for another year. There was no in-between. The people living in those cultures knew the difference between the actions of the immature and the actions of the mature. Once they were adopted into the "adult club" they put off the childish things, began to behave as an adult, and were given full rights and responsibilities of an adult. Talk about a day where everything changed!

Not so in modern America (as well as other industrialized nations). The period of life termed "adolescence" was defined as the transitional stage where children transformed into adults. This transition is no longer focused on an age, an event, or a task. Some argue it might take a child ten or twelve years to transition into adulthood – some argue that it takes even longer! Our culture still restricts the ages people can do certain things. You have to be old enough to get a job, drive a car, drink alcohol, vote in an election, get married, get a credit card, or rent a car. But we know that achieving an age threshold doesn't necessarily mean that someone is ready to do something. There are those who get a job before they're ready, are a danger to others on public highways, become easily addicted to controlled substances, aren't ready to selflessly invest into the life of another, properly handle money, or who can care for someone else's property. In America there certainly is more to being mature than the number of years we've been alive!

If maturity isn't defined by an age, and we don't have an event or task for a person to complete, then how do we know when someone has transitioned from childhood to adulthood? While there is much debate on exactly what steps an adolescent must take in order for them to be considered to be an adult, many psychologists agree that these three things are required for one to make the transition into adulthood:

1. They must be able to live on their own and financially support themselves.
2. They must be able to recognize that life is not all about themselves.
3. They must demonstrate a desire to work hard to make the world a better place because they're a part of it.

This understanding of maturity has little to do with age. I know of many older teenagers and young adults who are able to do the hard work to support themselves, who care about others around them, and who strive to improve the community they are in. Many times they are looked down upon because of their age. Most of them don't really care, they're too busy caring for the needs of their families and helping to meet the needs of those around them. I also know of others who are more than 30 who don't have jobs, who sit at home and watch TV or play video games all day, and who do nothing to better the lives of those around them. Many of them argue that their age allows them to make decisions about their own life. Some argue that they should receive respect and responsibilities simply because of their age – despite their living situations, lack of their contributions to society, or lack of concern for others around them.

Some argue that marketers have a strangle hold on our culture, stemming maturity for as long as possible because they realize that immature people are much easier to manipulate into purchasing their products. Immature people make more impulse purchases and abuse credit. Mature people plan their purchases and understand the benefits of a savings account. Immature people purchase things based on cultural popularity (because they're cool) and mature people first look at the utility of a purchase (Do I really need this? Will it meet the need I have?) Immature people go into a buying frenzy on Black Friday, buying things just because of the price, while mature people aren't conned into buying things they don't need or won't last long – no matter how great the price may be.

I could provide illustration after illustration regarding the practical differences between how mature people and immature people spend their money, their time, make priorities, care about others, and strive to leave a lasting, positive impact on the world around them. I'm sure you have great stories as well!

I believe that we could employ these same observations to help us determine when someone is in mature in Christ as well.

1. They must be able to feed themselves spiritually.
2. They must be able to recognize that the church is not there just for them.

3. They must demonstrate a desire to invest in the church (with their money, their time, their resources, their talents, and their spiritual gifts, etc.) to make it a better place because they're part of it.

Many churches are dealing with people who raise issues which begin with the words, "I'm not…" or "I don't think…" or "I want to…" These statements may be completed with the following statements:

- I'm not being fed.
- I don't like the worship music.
- I don't think the pastor (or ministry leader) is spending enough time with me.
- I don't think the church should spend time or money on…
- I want to go back to the way we did things 20 or 30 years ago.

Just about every pastor, elder, or board member can tell a story where they were part of lengthy debates over seemingly important topics such as:

- The color of paint on a wall
- The color of the cover of pew Bibles or Hymnals.
- The color of carpet.
- Pews vs chairs.
- Changing the pulpit or other things on the platform.
- The addition of new technology.
- The beginning of a new ministry.
- The closing of an existing ministry.
- What kind of worship style we should use on Sunday mornings.

While people's individual perspectives are valuable in any group discussion regarding every topic – from the color of carpet or paint on a wall to the development of new vision or ministries within a church – Jesus Christ's opinion should be the highest opinion in any such conversation. Too often we bypass the crucial step of engaging in listening prayer and allow popular opinion, or the opinion of one vocal person or group to make crucial decisions in church life and ministry. Quite often this is the result of immature Christians being given too much of a say regarding the matters of Christ's Holy Church.

How to Develop Maturity

Every parent knows that developing maturity is not a quick and easy process and that it can't be done just by focusing on head-knowledge. There is a marked difference between head-knowledge and wisdom, which is a great mark of maturity. Maturity must be developed by combining head-knowledge with experience, guided by those who are mature, cultured in an environment that allows for mistakes to be made, and leverages learning opportunities for growth opportunities.

Mature believers in Christ must take the responsibility of developing maturity in the lives of believers around them who are less mature. Immature believers in Christ cannot lead others to become mature in their faith because they have not yet achieved maturity in their own faith. They can spur one another on towards maturity, and walk down the discipleship journey with one another, but they cannot be the ones responsible for helping develop maturity in the lives of immature believers. They don't know what maturity looks like. They haven't experienced it in their own lives – how can they teach others to be mature?

The leaders of the early church got this concept. In Paul's letter to Titus he instructs Titus to teach others to be mature believers in Christ and then to encourage them to develop maturity in others around them.

> "But as for you, teach what accords with sound doctrine. Older men are to be sober-minded, dignified, self-controlled, sound in faith, in love, and in steadfastness. Older women likewise are to be reverent in behavior, not slanderers or slaves to much wine. They are to teach what is good, and so

train the young woman to love their husbands and children, to be self-controlled, pure, working at home, kind, and submissive to their own husbands, that the word of God may not be reviled." Titus 2:1-5.

Paul demonstrated the discipleship process that he taught Titus throughout his life and ministry. Most of Paul's New Testament writings convey his desire to introduce others to Christ and to disciple those who have chosen to follow Him. This model was very effective for the life and ministry of the early church. Through the power of the Holy Spirit the early church had a great influence over the world. The gospel message spread rapidly and thousands accepted the message of the new life anyone can have through relationship with Jesus Christ. The act of "accepting" this message wasn't the end of the road for them. They were taught to learn more and experience all that being a disciple of Christ involved. Although developing maturity was the intention of the apostles, and other church leaders, much of Paul's New Testament writings contained admonition regarding what immature church attenders were doing wrong and instruction on how to make it right. 2,000 years later we're still struggling to develop mature disciples. Note the contrast between some of the following differences between some contrasting attributes between mature and immature believers:

While certain points in the chart above may not apply to everyone in each category, and this list is certainly not exhaustive, these are some good indications of the maturity level of someone's walk with Christ. I realize that everyone is on a spiritual journey and we all have areas of our lives that need some improvement. I also realize that it takes time to develop spiritual disciplines, but I suggest that there are milestones of spiritual formation that can be seen in the lives of those who are striving to become more like Christ and indications in the lives of those who are not striving to become more like Christ.

Many followers of Christ struggle to move from the immature side of the chart to the mature side of the chart on their own. Their time in personal prayer and Bible study lead towards this goal, and the

Mature Believers	Immature Believers
Have a consistent personal devotional life	Have a sporadic or non-existent devotional life
Church attendance is a priority	Attend church when its convenient
Service is part of their discipleship	Aren't ready to serve
Give to the Lord generously	Struggle to find money to give to the work of the Lord
Have different passions from the world	Their lives look like those who are not Christians
Spend time in daily prayer	Pray sporadically
Regularly hear the voice of God	Struggle to hear the voice of God
Read deep spiritual books	Read watered-down spiritual books, if any
Can avoid false teachers	Can't discern good vs. false teaching
Know Biblical truth	Use popular spiritual jargon
Regularly use their spiritual gifts	Don't know their spiritual gifts
Live missionally	Don't live missionally
Are discipling others	Are not discipling others
Follow the leading of their leadership	Fight the leading of their leadership
Humbly confess their sin	Are caught in cycles of sin
Forgive others who have wronged them	Struggle to forgive others

working of the Holy Spirit calls them to maturity, but we must also develop a strategy to intentionally help people take steps to move from the personal traits found in immature believers to those of mature disciples of Jesus Christ.

Many issues that churches are experiencing in the areas of personal commitment, financial giving, leadership development, the establishment of vision, and the implementation of outreach would be solved if we intentionally worked with the Holy Spirit to develop maturity in the lives of those who attend. No, I would never suggest that we take the place of the Holy Spirit, but we need to have a better plan to work ***with the Holy Spirit*** to develop mature disciples of Christ.

What if I'm on the Wrong Side!

If you find yourself in many of the markers on the "Immature Christians" side of the above chart then I have few points of good news for you! First, everyone is immature at some point of their journey with Christ. If that's where you are, great! Now you know. If you strive to make the transition from the immature side to the mature side then read on. This book is going to help you with that.

Secondly, one of the signs of a healthy, growing relationship with God is that we go through seasons of assessment and growth. Knowing where you are is a first step to taking the next steps on your journey. Now you need to chart where you want to be and find a path to get there. Don't worry; God doesn't leave you to take this journey on your own. He meets us right where we are and leads us to our next steps. He quite often puts mature Christians in our life to help us on our journey. In fact, this book is about how we should help one another on our journeys together.

Let's say you're not feeling well and you go to the doctor to find out what's wrong. You might fear what the doctor has to say, the changes you might have to make in your life because of the diagnosis, medication that you'll have to take, or a surgery that might be impending. Even if you hear the doctor say the dreaded words, "you have cancer," knowing what you have is the first step towards getting better. You might have a tough road ahead, but knowing the right path to take to get you to where you want to be is much better than wandering down a path that is going nowhere – or in the wrong direction!

So, I encourage you to decide not to fight the diagnosis of your level of spiritual maturity. Let it be a step in a positive direction in this spiritual journey you'll be on for the rest of your life. Let it be part of the process the Holy Spirit uses to bring maturity to your relationship with Him!

Is Our Spiritual Formation Model Working?

This is a tough question that needs to be continually asked in every context of ministry. Many of us don't want to hear that ***our model isn't working***, but if we're not regularly assessing the effectiveness of our model and making changes as needed then we're probably just spinning our wheels in an ineffective model. Learning how to make an honest self-assessment, as well as making mid-course corrections as necessary, are hallmarks of a healthy disciple, a healthy church, or a healthy ministry. We could follow the way of the proverbial ostrich, sticking his head in the sand to ignore the problems around us, or we could make a humble, honest assessment of how well we're doing at making mature disciples of Jesus Christ and make the changes required through the leading and power of the Holy Spirit.

In Chapter 3 we'll take an in-depth look at the discipleship model that many churches employ and explore some suggestions on how leadership can make some changes to do a better job of making mature disciples of Jesus Christ who make more mature disciples of Jesus Christ.

Study Questions
Chapter 1
What Does a Disciple Look Like?

1. Have you ever considered that there is a difference between a convert and a disciple before?

2. To what extent have you been involved in making "converts to Christianity" in the past?

3. To what extent have you been involved in making "Disciples of Jesus Christ" in the past?

4. What do you think of PJ's working definition of disciple? What would you add if you were developing your own? What would you take away from his if you were developing your own?

5. As you look at your relationship with the church you attend, do you see yourself as a student in any of the services or ministries? How so?

6. How can you be a student without engaging in self-study through reading books?

7. How key do you think that assessment is in the process of discipleship?

8. Have you ever used a tool for assessment in the past? Which one? What did you learn about yourself?

9. Did you do the "Discipleship Assessment Sheet" – adapted from *Growing a Healthy Church*? What were some of your

observations from your own assessment?

10. Did you scale yourself on Engel's Evangelism Scale? Where did you fall?

11. What are some of your own personal observations on the steps required to move from immaturity to maturity?

12. Were you on the mature or immature side of the chart?

13. How do you respond to that?

14. Most people will not find themselves in every category of maturity. What steps are required in your life to move from immaturity to maturity in at least one section of the chart?

15. What's keeping you from taking those steps?

CHAPTER 2

DEVELOPING A PLAN FOR SPIRITUAL FORMATION

**"For those whom he foreknew he also predestined
to be conformed to the image of his Son,
in order that he might be the firstborn among many brothers.
And those whom he predestined he also called,
and those whom he called he also justified,
and those whom he justified he also glorified."
Romans 8:29-30.**

I believe the purpose of any Christian ministry, including the general purpose of the church, is to complete the Great Commandment (Matthew 22:35-40) and the Great Commission (Matthew 28:16-20). To love God, love others, share the Gospel Message, and make mature disciples who make mature disciples. This doesn't "just happen" by itself! No, mature disciples are best developed through an intentional disciple-making process.

Dan Spader studied the life and ministry of Jesus Christ to see if Jesus was intentional in His disciple-making process. He found that ***Jesus was very intentional*** throughout His disciple-making process. In his book, *Growing a Healthy Church*, Spader outlines Christ's process, highlights the key components He used, and suggests a model that the modern church can implement to make mature disciples the way that Jesus did. Spader argues that a ministry can accomplish this by creating a framework of ministry that has a balance between winning the lost, building the believer, equipping the worker, multiplying the leader, and sending the called ones.

To make disciples the way that Christ made disciples, this framework needs to be the vision and purpose of the church as a whole, as well as each individual ministry within the church. Each ministry of the church has to individually define how they are going to do each of these things in their own personal context. ***How*** they do these things will change from time to time. How each ministry accomplishes these aspects isn't important. ***That*** each ministry is doing these things is ***extremely important***. A healthy church wants to see women leading women to Christ, men leading men to Christ, families leading families to Christ, Sunday AM worship services leading people to Christ, students leading students to Christ, etc. Through all of this, the ministry leaders must focus on building disciples – not on building church attenders. Coming to Christ needs to be part of the discipleship process – not the targeted end of the process.

The framework needs to create an upward progression of maturity from a pre-Christian to a beginner in Christ to a mature disciple of Christ. This is done intentionally by developing ministries that help people take concerted steps of development in their discipleship. Each ministry leader has to define how their ministry is going to develop aspects of their ministry that fall into pre-determined stages of spiritual formation. Each ministry of the church needs to define these stages in their own context and create a plan to walk people through each of the stages.

This can happen within any particular ministry exclusive of other church ministries or by leveraging a variety of ministry opportunities in the church. For example, the youth ministry could use the worship service on Sunday mornings and the Sunday school hour as part of their disciple-building plan. Or they could develop their own Sunday morning program specifically designed to disciple students. While I prefer that families worship together on Sunday mornings, if a youth leader was able to provide a compelling argument for another plan to disciple students the elders and I would prayerfully consider it.

It's just not possible for a teacher, a pastor, or a ministry leader to develop spiritual formation for everyone at every ministry event. Each week in attendance we will find pre-Christians, new Christians, struggling Christians, and mature Christians. While a lesson (or sermon) can and should bring spiritual truth and practical application into the lives of everyone in the room, it's not possible for there to be deep, intentional spiritual formation taking place for every stage of discipleship in one sitting. We must have multiple learning opportunities available at a variety of discipleship stages outside of Sunday morning worship so that we can meet the spiritual needs of a variety of people.

A teacher who knows that they are speaking to pre-Christians is going to tailor their presentation to the crowd they are speaking to. A teacher who knows that they are speaking to mature Christians is going to tailor their presentation to the crowd they are speaking to. If they don't, in the first case, they will be speaking over the heads of those in attendance and little spiritual formation will be developed. In the latter, most of the material will be review and the crowd will leave with the thought, "I could have taught that lesson..." or "I'm not being fed and challenged."

The college metaphor gives us a great model to follow so that we don't teach over people's heads and we don't bore those who "could have taught our lesson!" I have chosen to use the college metaphor for this writing because I have seen it work very well in a variety of contexts of ministry. If you feel that this metaphor doesn't work well in your context, then the elders of the church, or the ministry leaders within a ministry, need to work on developing a metaphor that will work well for your context. No matter what metaphor is used, the principles of developing the structure for intentional spiritual formation are a must for any disciple, healthy church, or ministry.

Argument for the College Metaphor

I believe the modern college system has proven its ability to train a student to grasp a subject and prepare them for a career in a given field. It, like any other system, has its flaws, but outside of the apprentice model, I think that the college model has demonstrated that it is the most proven method for teaching and training that we offer in our modern culture. The church can learn many lessons from the model of teaching and intentional training that is demonstrated by the college method.

If leaders are willing to do an honest assessment, many churches would find that they are teaching the same material over and over again in a variety of program offerings. Sermons, Sunday school lessons, prayer groups, small groups, Bible studies, youth groups, and children's programs are teaching many of the same lessons in the same ways. Most lessons are lecture based and focused on "information transfer." There may be little emphasis on practical application on the lesson material being taught and few offerings that allow the students the opportunity to practice what they're being taught in an interactive manner in a mentoring learning environment.

I've been part of ministries who discovered that we were limiting our ability to graduate mature disciples of Jesus Christ because our lessons were similar in structure, similar in content, and weren't being practiced as they were taught. To change this we must ask questions about our purpose and practice. Jesus said to "make disciples," but what does a disciple look like? Don't we have to define what a disciple looks like before we set out to "make one?" How do we respond if what we're producing isn't what we intend to produce? A dedicated disciple of Christ, as well as a wise, healthy leader is going to ask these questions often and respond to the answers they find.

How the College System Operates

The undergrad college system has clearly defined four stages of learning designed to bring about a progression of learning and application of the learning in the life of its students. It works on a four-tier system of classes that are divided into 100, 200, 300, and 400 levels. The dynamics of each level are clearly defined. All professors and students know what to expect in each of the levels because the dynamics are clearly defined and closely adhered to.

Here is a basic break-down of the four levels in a college system:

100 Level – Beginning Level

Level of Learning
The professor is covering the basics of the subject. Most professors teaching this class are covering the same material across the entire college. The assumption is that the student is not familiar with this topic at all and needs to be educated on the basics of the area of study. Quite often a student who studied this area in high school will remark that most of the class was review to them, while someone who never took this area of study in high school is caught up to the student who did. This is where everyone learns the same terminology that will allow for more advanced learning at higher levels.

Student/Teacher Ratio

100-level classes offer a large student/teacher ratio. Many classes are held in large lecture halls. Most professors won't take attendance and grades are given based on testing only. In a large college there could be 500-1,000 students in a classroom with just one professor. In a smaller college there could be 30-50 students in the room.

Mentoring

There is almost a zero chance for a 100-level student to have one-on-one face time with a professor. Often students will be given the chance to meet with an assistant to the professor instead of meeting with the professor one-on-one. Most teachers will not meet their students face to face during the semester, nor will they remember their names after the class is done.

Learning Technique

Learning here is mostly lecture based or "information transfer." There is little to no opportunity for a student to ask questions or have interaction with the professor.

Application of Learning

Any application has to be presented in a general and generic format. Most of the application will apply to all of the students who are, or who have ever studied this topic. At this level it's rare for there to be a project for the student to work on. Most application within the topic is reserved for deeper levels of study.

Student Collaboration

There is little to no class interaction or student collaboration at this level. Students may meet to talk or study together outside of the classroom, but it's mostly to cut study time or help students who are not grasping the material.

200-Level – Intermediate Level

Level of Learning

The professor assumes the student has a good grasp of the 100-level materials. He/she is working to build upon that material and take the student deeper into the subject.

Student/Teacher Ratio

The student/teacher ratio is usually one half of that of the 100-level. In a large college this class could have 200 students in it. In a smaller college there may be 15-20 in the room. Professors may try to become acquainted with students, but it's still easy for a student to sneak under the radar at this level.

Mentoring

Most teachers will offer office hours for 200-level classes. They will have time to have a significant conversation with one or two students from a class. Most teachers will remember basic things about their students and will be identifying potential students to invest in during the deeper levels ahead. But, still, for the most part, there is little to no mentoring taking place at the 200-level.

Learning Technique

Learning here is still mostly lecture based or "information transfer." The teacher is beginning to take more questions, but still has to "keep to the material" for the most part.

Application of Learning

Most application is still presented in a general or generic format. At this level the professor may begin to personalize application based on student interests, but for the most part the focus is still on "general application" principles. Most personal application within the topic is reserved for the two deeper levels of study.

Student Collaboration

Class interaction and collaboration may be introduced, but in limited ways. There might be one or two projects for small groups to work on throughout the semester, but in a larger college there still may not be any collaboration at all. Students may meet outside of the classroom for study groups, or to help other students who are struggling with the material, but this isn't intentionally designed into the class structure.

300-Level –Advanced Level

Level of Learning

At this level the professor assumes that the 100 and 200 materials have weeded out those who aren't able to comprehend the topic – or who aren't interested in continuing its study. This is the first level where the professor begins to invest in the student on a more intimate level. A command of 100- and 200 level material is assumed and not covered. It's time to strap in and go deeper into the topic.

Student/Teacher Ratio

This is again about half of the 200-level student teacher ratio. Now, even in larger colleges, classes are capped in the 15-30 student range. Office hours are offered and students are encouraged to take advantage of them for deeper conversations and study.

Mentoring

At the 300-level professors are identifying students who will stand out and are investing more time and personal access into their learning process.

Learning Technique

Learning often transitions from a lecture-based approach to more of a guided-learning approach. Homework assignments, research projects, and collaborative efforts become a major part of the learning plan. The assignments are discussed in class and the learning path becomes more fluid based on the direction the discussions take.

Application of Learning
At this level the professor will allow for personal application based on a student's interest. Rather than learn broad, basic application, customized, specific applications are explored and researched.

Student Collaboration
At this level the learning experience becomes more collaborate. Students interact with the teacher during each class and most professors give their students assignments that require full class participation and probably involve small group collaboration. A large part of their grade may depend on group-based projects.

400-Level – Expert Level

Level of Learning
At this level the professor assumes the student is going to use the material covered as a chosen career field. The material is designed to challenge the student and prepare them to use the knowledge and its application on a regular basis.

Student/Teacher Ratio
Here the student/teacher ratio is the closest to one-on-one that the student will experience, unless they continue on to higher education levels. At this level most students will have the opportunity to get to know their professors in a personal way.

Mentoring
Teachers are investing personally into the lives of their students at this level. As they realize that this is going to be their students' career field teachers invest to help them succeed as much as possible. Some teachers take a personal investment in the outcome of the student's education and career.

Learning Technique
There is very little lecture taking place at this level. Learning is mostly done in collaborative means. A student's entire grade may be

based on one or two projects they do on their own, or as a collaborate effort with the entire class – or as small groups within the class.

Application of Learning
At this level, the application can be tailored to the specific interests of the class or to each individual student. By this time class offerings are specialized into specific areas of application of the field of study and customized areas of application can be achieved.

Student Collaboration
At this level student collaboration is a daily thing. Students may be given assignments to research and teach certain aspects to the rest of the class. The teacher may step aside almost completely and allow the students to serve as the teachers as he or she steps into more of a coaching role.

It Only Takes Four Years

At the end of the four years a student who has successfully completed the progression of study that has been designed by the college will be ready to step into the real-world and apply the lessons learned in a practical way.

All of this is accomplished within four years. By following the intentional system, the student has made a concerted effort to cover the material required to bring them from a cursory knowledge of a subject to be well on their way to becoming an expert in it. They have invested a lot of time, a lot of money, and a lot of effort. As they look back on the past four years they can see the amazing progress they've made in many areas of their lives.

Of course, for some of us, this process takes us more than four years. We might have to take a break in our studies. We might have to take a step back and repeat a class or two. We might have to reassess a study or career path. That's okay. The system is designed for that too!

Masters and Doctorate Levels

Some of the markings of higher education are that classes are much more fluid, done in very small groups, and almost completely mentor driven. Most of the coursework is done by the student on his or her own, or in very small collaborative groups. This allows the coursework to be completely customizable for the specific applications of the learning for each student. At these levels the student must take the initiative in the learning process. If they're not willing to do the work they're simply not going to be able to accomplish the degree.

Core Differences Between the College System and the Church System

Let's contrast this intentional learning progression designed by colleges to what a student will find in many church situations:

Many Sunday morning presentations aren't working to bring the student along on a progressive learning curve. They're mostly stand-alone lessons, or a short series, designed to convey one particular topic and/or point. Then the teacher or preacher moves onto the next point or the next sermon series. These new points or series are often unrelated to the topic or study just completed. There are no planned "merge points" along the way. New students coming in the door are expected to merge on their own. They may be overwhelmed with the material being presented, but there probably isn't a plan to help them catch up to the rest of the class.

Many Sunday school classes work independently from the others – as well as the material being presented during the Sunday morning service. There isn't an intentional learning progression from one group to another. A student may hear the same lessons or points from year to year as they progress through a department or graduate from one department to another. They may even hear the same material presented in the Sunday morning worship service and in Sunday school on some weeks.

Many small groups are designed to work independently of the church as a whole. Here learning can be much more interactive, but again, with no learning plan a student might be learning the same things they learned in Sunday morning worship and/or in Sunday school.

Sometimes the teacher brings the lesson material back to the very beginning whenever there is a new person added to the mix. Rather than create a way for the new person to catch up outside of the group, the teacher defaults back to the beginning of their lesson plan so that everyone in the class is on the same page. In a healthy church, there will always be more new people coming in the door, so this teacher will regularly reset to the beginning – and may never make it to the end of their lesson plan. A teacher who uses the large group teaching time to keep everyone on the same page will lose the interest of those who have been there the whole time.

I experienced this myself as I was teaching a Sunday school class for high school students. We were studying the book *Experiencing God* by Blackaby. The joke in the class was that every time a visitor walked in the door we defaulted back to a lesson covering the "Seven Realities of Experiencing God." I found that my entire lesson time was taken up by reviewing these seven realities and how far we've made it in the class up until that point. After having new people come in the door each week for a couple of months a couple of students who were the core of the group approached me with their complaint. "If you don't stop going over the same 'Seven Realities of Experiencing God' and finish this book we're quitting the class." Yeah, that got my attention.

Many churches don't offer "hands on" learning opportunities – places where prayer, evangelism, apologetics, or spiritual gifts are put into action. Some churches offer these things to those ***inside*** of the church, but few offer opportunities to put these lessons into action ***outside*** of the church building.

The lack of an intentional, church-wide learning plan means that a church isn't going to be able to "graduate students" with the skills necessary to succeed in the "Christian career" field. These students are going to struggle to figure out how to apply the head knowledge they have gained in a personal and practical way. While general principles and application will be presented through sermons and lessons, the lack of one-on-one mentoring that 300-level, 400-level, and higher learning opportunities afford leave them struggling to apply these principles in their own personal "real world" experiences.

Some of the statistics coming from the Barna Group show us that most people who call themselves Christians don't read their Bibles, pray, or make church attendance a priority in their lives. Most don't share their faith, have a biblical world view, or use biblical principles in making day-to-day decisions in their lives. They are struggling in the "Christian career field." We must change this unsettling trend!

Leaders must look at ***equipping*** as a primary role of their leadership. We must do more than tell our students what they need to know, but we must tell them how to develop spiritual disciplines, coach them on using them, and help them learn to apply what they're learning on their own to their own personal experiences. This simply can't be done through a typical Sunday morning church experience. We have to do more.

Paul understood this as he wrote to churches and leaders in the New Testament. In Ephesians 4 he writes that his intention is to equip God's people for works of service so that they would become mature believers and be effective in service. Much of what I see around me in the modern church model fails to equip and struggles to develop the crucial spiritual discipline of effective service, both within the Body of Christ and within the community in which the church resides. Most of church ministry is designed as a "come and listen to what I have to say" presentation. It allows for one or two leaders to make it to the top of the ministry ladder. They then define the majority of their ministry as "come to hear what I know." This develops a competitive atmosphere, as leaders strive to keep their "top level" positions, and those who wish to help them may be seen as competitors. Many of these same leaders say, "I wish we could get more people involved." But they don't realize that their church structure may very well be the thing that is prohibiting more people from becoming involved. They're not equipping them to serve and they're not developing opportunities for those who are equipped to serve.

So, What Do We Do?

If we wish to intentionally work with the Holy Spirit to develop spiritual maturity in the life of anyone we are discipling – either one-on-one or through a church or ministry – then we have to develop various venues and dynamics for spiritual formation to occur. Just as an accomplished college student has to graduate from 100 classes to 200 classes; from 200 classes to 300 classes; from 300 classes to 400 classes; and then pursue deeper study, an accomplished disciple of Jesus Christ must graduate through spiritual formation offerings at church. For him or her to do so, leaders must intentionally create offerings with a similar dynamic to what is offered at a typical college. We might even title classes with the 100, 200, 300, and 400 titles so that prospective students know the level of learning our classes and programs offer.

We must learn to ask questions such as:

- Where does a seeker go to have their questions answered?
- What does a mature disciple of Jesus Christ look like?
- What process is required to develop a mature disciple of Christ?
- What spiritual disciplines does a disciple need to learn and apply in their lives?
- How can we teach and mentor these disciplines?
- How can we develop hands-on learning opportunities?
- What training is being offered for those who are interested in serving?
- What is the process for someone to be an elder, a board member, or ministry leader?

- Are leaders incorporating an apprenticeship approach to eventually replace their own leadership positions? If not, why not?
- How long does it take to properly train someone to be a disciple of Jesus Christ?

There are no doubt dozens more questions that will come up as we begin to answer questions like these. Once we begin to answer these questions we have to prayerfully strategize ways to begin to implement them into our church or ministry structures.

Intentional Spiritual Formation

I've embraced an intentional spiritual formation approach in my own personal life and ministry that closely resembles that of the college metaphor. Here's how it works:

The 100-level is church on Sunday morning. This is where one speaker can teach a lot of people all at once – people who happen to be at a variety of different places in their knowledge of Scripture. We cover the basics here, hoping that when people hear the basics they will be interested in going deeper. This is a great place for those who already know the basics to worship and help serve those who are learning the basics. When someone expresses a desire to go deeper, we invite them to go to the next level…

The 200-level is Sunday school (or Sunday school-like classes). Here one teacher is able to go deeper than the 100-level. Class sizes are smaller, teaching time is longer, and there is opportunity for questions to be asked and answered. In most classes homework is offered for those who wish to study deeper. Classes are able to be offered according to more specific interests, such as a specific book of the Bible, a topic from the Bible, or a study through a book about applying biblical principles into our modern culture. If people are interested in doing a study that goes deeper, or involves even more interaction, they are invited to go to the next level…

The 300-level is small groups. Groups have more time together than Sunday school classes offer. They involve a deeper dependence on spiritual disciplines such as prayer, Bible study, worship, teaching, hospitality, and discernment. Also, there is a much greater opportunity for question asking and personal input into the lesson-based discussion. Participants are expected to do homework throughout the week and come to meetings prepared for the discussion. Some groups are able to share the leadership role – either by allowing different people to lead different areas, or by rotating people through various leadership positions. I also offer some 300-level leadership development options that operate as a combination of 200- and 300-level dynamics. When a student is interested in going even deeper, they are invited to go to the next level…

The 400-level is meeting with people one-on-one. Here the learning plan is custom tailored to exactly what the student requires. Homework is extensive. Radical learning is fostered in a learning environment that is only limited by the amount of effort the student is willing to put into it. If you're interested in gaining a better understanding of exactly how a 400-level learning environment can operate, then read on. That's what this book is all about!

Study Questions
Chapter 2
Developing a plan for spiritual formation

1. Have you ever served as a teacher in a class or ministry at church? Tell your story.

2. How did you approach the question of what level of discipleship to target in your lessons? Did you target pre-Christians, baby Christians, or those more mature in their faith?

3. Did you ever struggle with an attempt to teach them all at the same time? How so?

4. PJ took seven pages to outline the college metaphor. What are some of your own personal observations with this metaphor?

5. How can you compare your own personal church involvement with the college metaphor? In what ways do you see a parallel though process in the development of learning opportunities? Or is there more of a disconnect from this theory of education?

6. Have you ever felt that a teacher was covering material that was "way over your head?" Tell of the circumstance and your reaction to it.

7. Have you ever felt that a teacher was covering material that you could have covered? Tell of the circumstance and your reaction to it.

8. On page 65 PJ outlines his personal ministry philosophy regarding the implementation of the college metaphor. How

well does this resonate with your experiences? Have you experienced another implementation of it that worked to build spiritual formation in your life? Tell your story.

9. Have you ever been part of a learning environment at church where you had to do homework? Tell the story.

10. Have you ever been involved in a one-on-one discipleship relationship with a spiritual mentor? How well did this build into your spiritual life?

CHAPTER 3

BUILDING A LEADERSHIP STRUCTURE

"I appeal to you therefore, brothers, by the mercies of God,
to present your bodies as a living sacrifice,
holy and acceptable to God, which is your spiritual worship.
Do not be conformed to this world,
but be transformed by the renewal of your mind,
that by testing you may discern what is the will of God,
what is good and acceptable and perfect."
Romans 12:1-2.

As we begin to gather people together to form a local church or ministry and work to develop a plan for a structure to develop spiritual formation in the lives of those who attend we must wrestle with the question of what kind of leadership model we are going to incorporate. Many churches incorporate a pulpit-driven leadership model. It involves a pastor who is the top dog of the church. He or she may work with a group of elders, or a board, but for the most part the pastor is the one who calls the shots. The pastor is the one who does most of the preaching and teaching. The pastor is the one who designs the plan for spiritual formation, leadership development, vision, and priorities of the church – or the lack thereof.

Drawing Circles

There are inherent limitations in a pulpit-driven leadership model. Let me try to explain this concept to you by drawing circles.

Let's say that the top circle represents me as a pastor. Aren't I a good-looking, symmetrical kind of a guy? Ha. Ha.

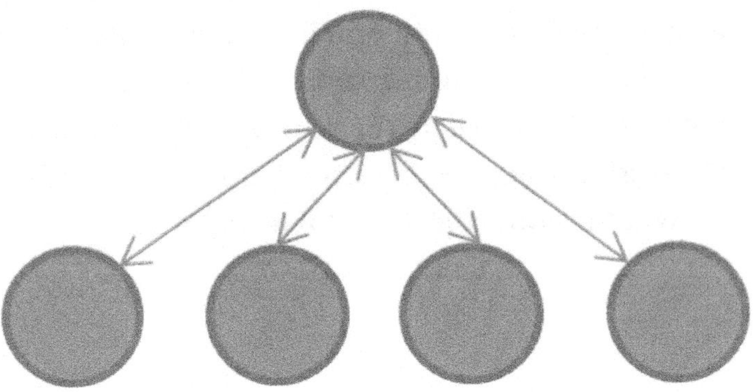

As a pastor I am a disciple of Jesus Christ and I am intentionally placing myself in a position of influence over others who are interested in knowing more about Jesus Christ. I'm praying for the others, serving them, demonstrating Christ's love to them, sharing the Gospel message with them, and they eventually come to know Jesus Christ as their Savior. Then, I work to teach them what following Christ looks like. I teach them how to read and study the Bible, how to pray, how to discover and use spiritual gifts, etc.

Those in the second row experience a life change as Christ does His amazing work in their lives and they begin to take steps of spiritual formation that are on the positive side of the Engel Scale. At some point, their spiritual formation prompts them to influence others around them for the sake of the Kingdom. They invite others to come and meet me, because I am the person who influenced them, and it leads to the next image.

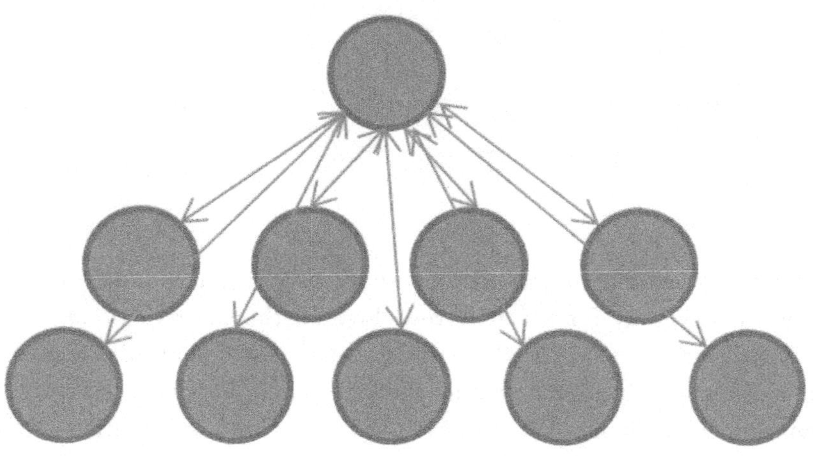

I am now ministering to those I led to Christ and their friends. I am praying for the new row, loving on them, serving them, sharing the Gospel message with them, and this row eventually come to know Jesus Christ as their Savior. I then work to teach them what following Christ looks like. All the while I am still ministering to those who initially came to Christ. I now teach the new row how to read and study the Bible, how to pray, how to discover and use spiritual gifts, etc.

They too experience a life change and take that life-changing message to others in their life. They bring more people to come and meet the person who influenced them and it leads to the next image.

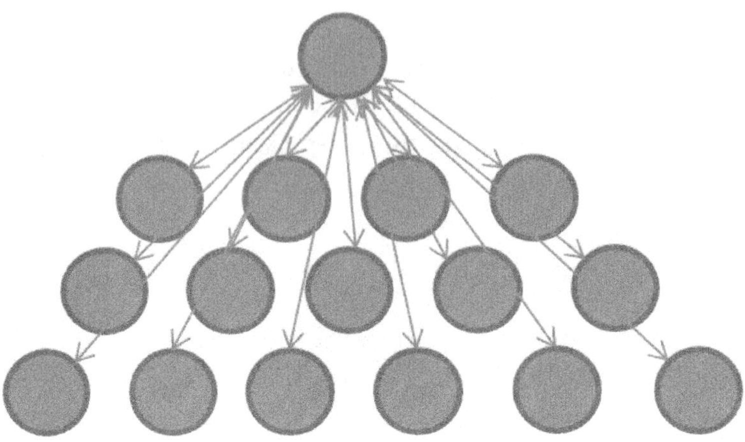

Having developed a successful process by which I am able to influence others, I now pray for the new row, love on them, serve them, share the Gospel message with them, and the new row eventually comes to know Jesus Christ as their Savior as well. Then, I strive to show them what following Christ looks like. All the while I am still ministering to those in rows one and two. The new row is invited to join the others as I teach everyone how to read and study the Bible, how to pray, how to discover and use spiritual gifts, etc.

They too experience a life change and take that life-changing message to others in their life. They bring others to come and meet the person who influenced them and it leads to the next image.

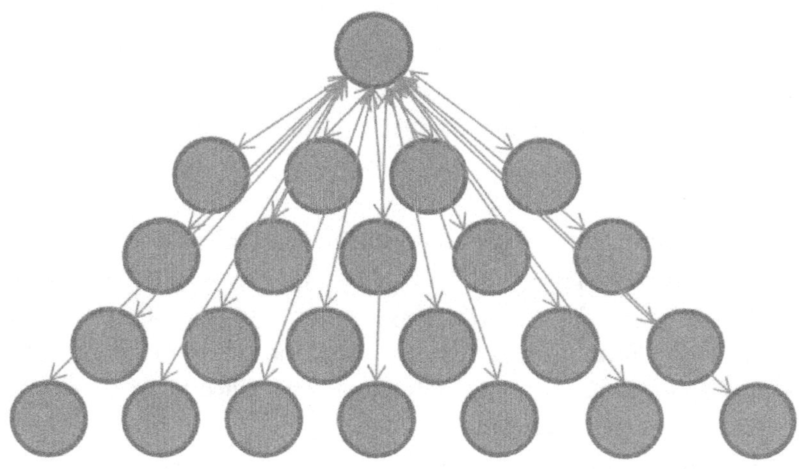

And so on… and so on…and so on.

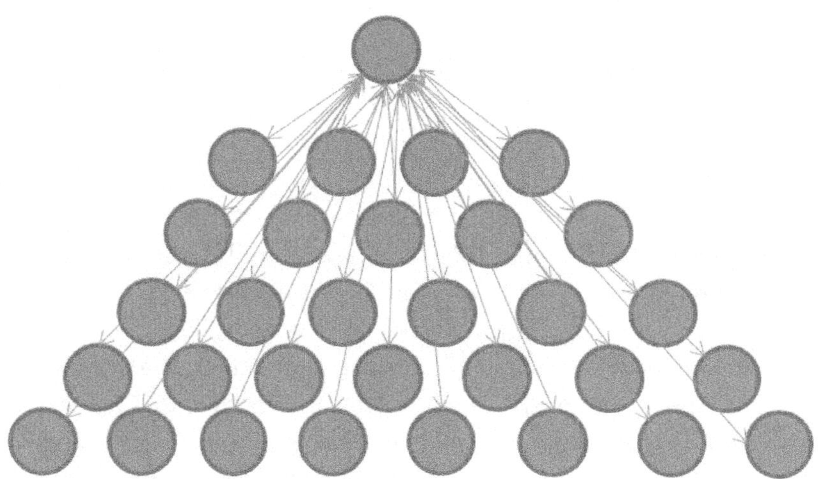

Does this image look familiar to you? It's the model of the modern church! A pastor, a Sunday school teacher, or a ministry leader has a great influence over a group of people and these people are dependent on the pastor, the Sunday school teacher, or ministry leader to help them grow in their faith. Notice that the arrows only go between the pastor and the people. There are no arrows going from person in the crowd to person in the crowd. People continue to bring others into the church so that they can be influenced by the pastor or teacher. The pastor bears most of the responsibility to meet with them, to pray for them, to teach them about Jesus, to counsel them, etc.

This model has some inherent limitations. The pastor, or ministry leader, is only one person! He or she can only meet with so many people at a time. As we talked about last chapter, there is only so much spiritual formation that can occur in a one-to-many model. As this model continues to grow it leads to the place where one person can't keep up with the needs of everyone! For a time people are patient, willing to wait their turn to have some one-on-one time with the person who discipling them (the pastor or ministry leader), but eventually, as more growth occurs, some find that the pastor or ministry leader doesn't have the time to meet their needs and they find another church to attend where they can get more one-on-one time and attention.

How Many People Can We Know?

Robin Dunbar was a British anthropologist who, in the 1990s, postulated that any one person can keep track of about 150 different people in their life (Dunbar). These are people who you know well enough to remember things like birthdays, family members' names, shared interests – and people who you have personal experiences with. These are not the "acquaintances" you bump into from time to time, your long-ago friends from High School, or all of those friends you might have on your Facebook whom you rarely talk to. It's not the total number of people you've met, you've known in your lifetime, or you're related to. These are the people who are playing some sort of an active role in your life currently. I know, the number is subjective to a variety of factors, and it will vary from person to person, but let's work with the number that Dunbar suggested.

Let's say that the average person has about 50 family members and friends that take up part of the 150 they're keeping track of and that another 50 is taken up with work or school connections. That leaves us with 50 connections we can make in a place like a church. Again, I know this is subjective, and it will vary, but let's just work with it for the sake of this example.

No matter how large a church may be, from 50 people to 60,000 people, each person can only realistically keep track of about 50 people in the church. You can only know so many names, so many birthdays, so many family facts, favorite sports teams, etc. Because people in groups tend to want to personally know and be known by others in groups, and in many cases want to know ***everyone in a group***, churches have tended to be limited to a size where any one person can maintain connections with most of the others in the group.

A Barna Group study done in 2003 reported that the average Protestant church size in America is 89 adults. The report said that 60% of churches have less than 100 adults and that only 2% have over 1,000 adults in attendance.

With the weekly attendance numbers at churches like Saddleback 22,000, Willow Creek 25,000, Calvary Chapel 18,000, and the Gateway Church 27,000 (along with dozens of other churches reporting more than 5,000 in attendance each week) – there have to be thousands of churches with attendance less than 50 per week in order to create an average attendance of 89 per week. It's easy to see that the vast majority of churches in America have a weekly attendance of somewhere around 50 adults.

I suggest that there are two reasons why most churches have about 50 adults in attendance:

1. Most people want to know everyone who goes to church with them.

2. Most people want the pastor to be the one who cares for everyone in the church.

While there is nothing inherently wrong with either of these things, they tend to become factors that limit church growth rather than factors that enhance church growth. A church must develop ministries that allow people to connect on smaller levels if they are going to grow beyond numbers where everyone can know everyone else. This is usually done through small groups and targeted Bible studies or ministries.

In this pulpit-driven ministry model someone must come to the pastor anytime they have questions, need counseling, or want to take further steps to become involved in the church. The pastor's schedule becomes the bottle-neck that limits the number of people who can be ministered to each week. I know that I've come to realize that I've been the bottle -neck for further church growth a number of times and had to wrestle with the process of giving responsibilities over to others so that I could stop prohibiting church growth.

In the average church, for the most part, the pastor is able to maintain a connection with everyone in the church because most people don't need personal attention every week. There are some who may call each day; and there may be some situations that require many days or weeks of the pastor's attention, but for the most part emergencies in a congregation are spread out so that the pastor can manage them one at a time. Still, this often leads to burn-out in the life of the pastor, stresses on his family, and will often lead people in the congregation to leave the church in search of a church where they will receive more on-on-one time with the pastor.

If you take the pastor out of this model the church experiences crisis (sometimes the crisis is extreme). They usually won't have anyone who is able to step forward and take the pastor's place. This model may cause the church to go into a hibernation mode until they are able to find another pastor to jump start its ministries once again. During that time many will find another church to attend where they can gain more pastoral attention.

Doing Better than Average

You might look at the numbers I presented above and think, "Wow, our church has about 100 in attendance. We're better than the average." I have two thoughts for you! First, are you okay with being above average? Didn't Christ demand that we invest our all in His Kingdom? Doesn't He deserve us to strive to lead a church that is so much more than "above average?" I think so!

Secondly, assuming that your church only has one pastor on staff, your church might be "above average" simply because there is a retired pastor in your congregation, someone who has gone through some Bible training, or someone who is going through some pastoral training now. Perhaps they've gone to the pastor and said, "I know that you've got a lot on your plate. How about letting me head up Sunday school, the visitation ministry, leading small groups, or something else that would free up some of your time." In essence, you have two of these pyramids existing in your church. The people in the pews can look to one of two leaders to be their shepherd. They're going to be able to lead about 50-100 people each, thereby doubling the amount of people they can care for as a church. You might be able to have more people around week to week, but if both of these people are taken out of the scenario now you have to watch two pyramids fall apart until new leaders can take their place.

Discipleship Leadership Model

Let me present another model to you. It's a leadership model that is based on biblical discipleship. In this model the circle on the left represents that same disciple of Jesus Christ who puts himself/herself in a position of influence over others who are interested in knowing more about Jesus Christ. That person prays for the others, serves them, loves on them, shares the Gospel message with them, and they eventually come to know Jesus Christ as their Savior. Then, that person works to teach them what following Christ looks like. They teach the others how to read and study the Bible, how to pray, how to discover and use their spiritual gifts, etc.

For the sake of this discussion, that person is still me. I'm still playing the part of a pastor, I'm still working on developing discipleship in the lives of others, but there are a few key differences in how I go about it! Trust me. You'll want to read on...

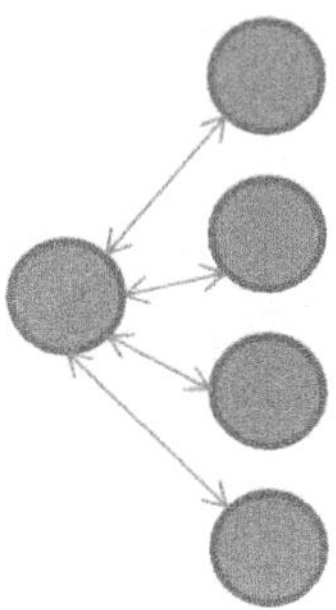

At first this model looks a lot like the pulpit-driven one. The difference in the discipleship model is that the person on the left intentionally teaches each of the people they're discipling how to have the same kind of a discipleship influence in the lives of others. Rather than encouraging them to invite others to come and meet me so that I can disciple them too, I teach them how to have that same pattern of love and commitment in the lives of others around them. The following image represents how their influence begins to spread.

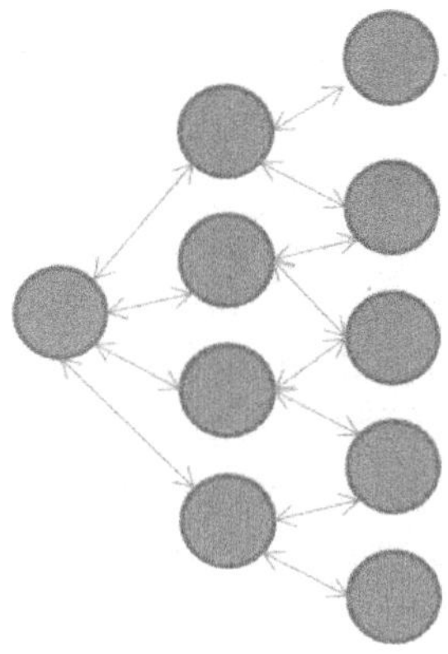

Notice the difference in the arrows. Rather than pointing everyone back to me, they take the responsibility of discipling those around them. They are praying for each other, sharing God's love with each other, teaching each other, answering questions, helping them become part of the Body of Christ, and working together to be used for the great things God has planned for His body – together.

In this model, when someone has questions about God, or practical needs that have to be met, they can depend on the person who is discipling them. When that person doesn't have the answers to their questions, or needs guidance in meeting their needs, he or she can then turn to me (the pastor) – as the one who is discipling them. I can then teach them, as the person I'm discipling, and that person can then pass that information down a level. In this scenario the person I'm discipling has learned new information about God, or ways to meet tangible needs, and has been the one who is ministering to the one they are discipling. Now they are better able to respond without help the next time these same questions or needs come up because I've taught them how to respond – rather than going around them to respond to the person they're discipling on my own.

As these new people experience a life change, and take that life-changing message to others, they depend on the person who discipling them to help them minister to others in their life. They are not dependent on the pastor – they are dependent on the person who is discipling them. This then leads to the next image.

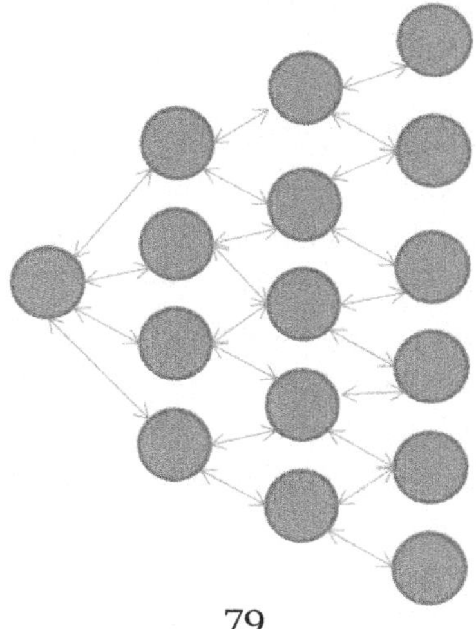

Now, as each of the levels of people are added, there are more and more people being trained in deeper discipleship knowledge and skills – and more people actively using those skills to disciple others. As each of them work to reach out to and disciple others, the church is able to grow, the leadership responsibilities are shared by those one level up, and the pastor is able to maintain a focus on those he is primarily discipling.

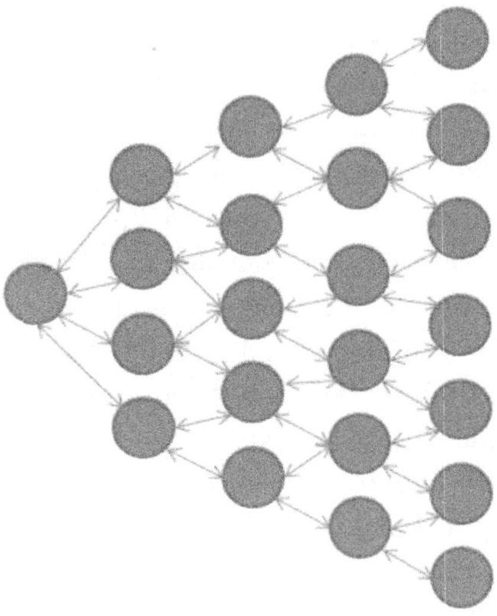

The limitations of the pulpit-driven model simply do not exist within the discipleship model. The majority of the pastor's time continues to be invested in a few, who are in turn investing in a few more, who are in turn investing in a few more, etc. There is no limit to the number of people who can be reached, discipled, and cared for in this model.

In addition, as you take any one of these people out of the structure, others are trained to replace them, either in personal discipleship, or in ministry leadership. In fact, a church that has developed this discipleship model can even cut off a section of those in discipleship relationships and plant a new church with them. This new church will have healthy leadership from the start, a discipleship mentality, along with a healthy leadership growth process inherent in their DNA. The original church misses the people who are being grafted to be part of the new plant, but they have layers of leadership designed into their structure and new leaders are eager to step up into the vacant positions.

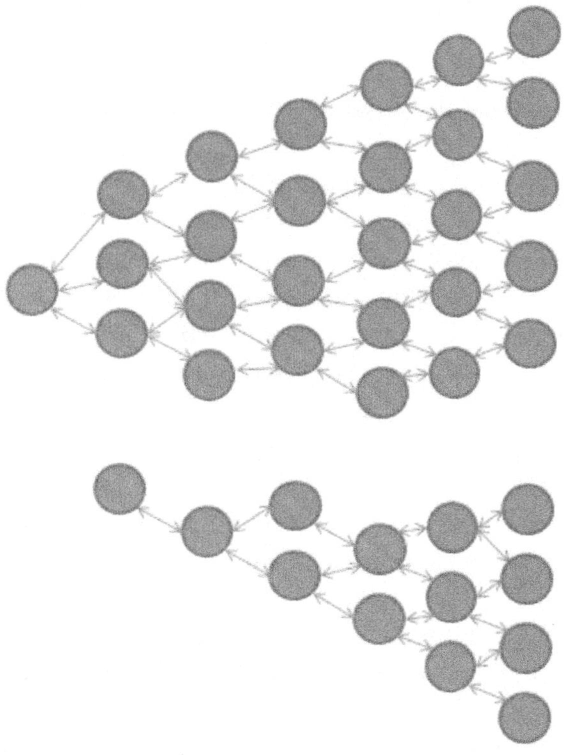

Don't get me wrong. The pastor or ministry leader is still a necessary part of the church in this leadership model. He or she still has influence over the whole church through their preaching and teaching, but they're sharing the responsibility and privilege of discipling others. As they disciple their leaders they are developing pastoral leadership discipleship skills in their lives, and they are seeing the fruit of their investment in the lives of others.

What Did Jesus Do?

Which of these models did Jesus employ in His life and ministry? If this isn't a rhetorical question for you, the answer is "The discipleship model!!!" A close look at how Jesus spent His time in ministry will find that the amount of time He spent with people ***increased*** as their commitment to Him increased.

- He spent the least amount of time with the crowd.
- He spent more time with His believers.
- He spent even more time with the core believers. This would have been people like Mary, Mary, Martha, and Lazarus.
- He spent even more time with His disciples. This group of disciples was first developed as He taught in the synagogue before He began His formal ministry. As He began His public ministry the number of His disciples was pared down to the final 12.
- He spent even more time with Peter, James, and John.
- We could argue that He spent the most time with either Peter or John.

Notice the spiritual benefits from Christ's investment of time and discipleship lessons. The crowd was the one who cried out to crucify Him. Many of those who claimed to be His believers weren't willing to make the sacrifices He called them to. His disciples, turned apostles, through the indwelling of the Holy Spirit, changed the world. Most of them were obedient to His plan for their lives even to the point of dying for their faith. As we read the book of John, the epistles that Peter wrote, and the history of the early church, we see the great benefit of the time that Christ spent with Peter and John.

Jesus invited anyone into this close, personal relationship with Him. It came with expectations and qualifications. Only those who were willing to meet those expectations were able to benefit from the close, personal one-on-one time with Him.

We Can See This Fruit Too

As a pastor, I've seen the great fruit that comes from spending time intentionally discipling the leadership of the church and asking them to spend time discipling others as well. I've set expectations and qualifications that are patterned after those Christ demanded of His disciples. Those who are willing to strive to meet them have benefitted from the time we've spent together, and those they've discipled have benefitted from the time they've spent with them as well.

Putting this model of leadership into action has caused me to ask the question, "How long does it take to make disciples of Christ?"

Study Questions
Chapter 3
Building a Leadership Structure

1. Which of the two leadership structure models have you experienced the most in your life?
2. How have you experienced the top down model?
3. What benefits and limitations did you observe with this model?
4. How have you experienced the side-by-side leadership model?
5. What benefits and limitations did you observe with this model?
6. How many people do you think you know in your life?
7. How many of those people are you able to really keep track of?
8. How do you feel when someone "slips through the cracks" and you lose track of them?
9. Have you ever been part of a new church plant or new ministry plant that was developed by grafting a group of people from an existing church or ministry? What was your experience like?

CHAPTER 4

HOW LONG DOES IT TAKE TO MAKE DISCIPLES?

**"Which is why I suffer as I do.
But I am not ashamed, for I know whom I have believed,
and I am convinced that he is able to guard until that Day
what has been entrusted to me.
Follow the pattern of the sound words that you have heard from me,
in the faith and love that are in Christ Jesus.
By the Holy Spirit who dwells within us,
guard the good deposit entrusted to you."
2 Timothy 1:12-14.**

When I ask most Christians how they're being discipled, they reply, "I go to church." When I ask most church leaders what their discipleship process looks like, they mention sermons, Sunday school lessons, and some mention small groups. I rarely hear Christians mention doing their own personal Bible study, engaging in personal worship, or practicing listening prayer as part of their spiritual formation plan. I almost never hear someone mention a one-on-one discipleship relationship with a spiritual mentor. While sermons, Sunday school lessons, and small group meetings are all good things – and they are a crucial part of discipleship – they are all accomplished in groups of people of various sizes, and most of them will take a long time to make disciples. Those looking to be discipled have to find the group they can fit in with and then they will learn at the pace of the leader. What happens if there isn't a group they fit into? What happens if they lag behind or want to go ahead of the pace set by the leader? What do they do then?

For the most part, the modern church model is ***a long-term discipleship model***. We have developed a system that takes twenty or thirty years to make a disciple. We've developed a system that says, "If you want to become a disciple of Jesus you have to come to church on Sunday morning, attend Sunday school, come to mid-week prayer services, and be part of a small group." Many of those designing the process don't really have an "end game" in mind. They haven't wrestled with the questions of what a disciple of Christ looks like or the process involved. They're just "doing church" and hoping that disciples are being made in the process. Many count church attendance and money in the bank as the primary measuring sticks of a successful church ministry. Many of them have few solutions to offer when attendance is waning and their bank account is dwindling other than "attract more people" or "convince more to give."

Those who attend most churches look at the leaders in the church as the ones who are supposed to do most of the discipling. Therefore, the pastor and ministry leaders must do most, if not all, of their discipling through preaching and teaching. They simply don't have the time to meet with people any other way. Our discipleship has become a lecture-based, knowledge-based, participant-based discipleship model. There is little "doing" outside of bringing your Bible and following along through the sermon. Most of the work done in a church is done by a select few within the church, mostly paid staff and a few ministry leaders. Many people in the church like this approach because it's more comfortable to learn in large groups than it is to learn by engaging in self-study. In many cases it's building a crowd in attendance each Sunday, but an honest look would find that it's not doing enough to make disciples of Jesus Christ.

It's so hard for a preacher or teacher to cover the ***whole Bible*** in their lesson plan. If a pastor preached through the entire Bible by covering one chapter a week, it would take him 23 years to preach from cover to cover!!! (There are 1,189 chapters in the Bible.) If he put his "preaching through the Bible plan" on hold for a topical sermon on Christmas, Easter, and Mother's Day, then it will take him more than 30 years to preach through the Bible. It could take a Sunday school teacher twice as long if he or she incorporated discussion in their lessons.

Even if I embraced the thought that it would be enough to cover the entire Bible just once in one person's lifetime (which I do not embrace), I see that this model would only work with a static group of people. One group of people, unchanging, who begins at the very first lesson, who is there for every lesson, and who sees the interconnectivity of points from week to week. A teacher struggles to be effective when students aren't there all the time and can't really see the connectivity between the teacher's lessons from session to session. When you introduce the fact that people will move away from the church and new people will be introduced into the church, the teacher of the long-term model struggles to keep everyone on the same page. I think we're better off admitting that it's just not possible.

While I admit this model of Sunday morning sermons, Sunday school classes, and small groups could be a feasible approach to developing mature disciples of Christ, an honest assessment of where we are in the modern church in America shows us that this model simply isn't working. Many churches are experiencing decline. Many churches are aging without replacing older members with those from younger generations. Many have become irrelevant institutions amidst a culture that is rapidly becoming post-Christian. Rather than thrust ourselves into a hostile culture to pull the lost from the dying tide, we're closing our doors and hoping to ride out the storm, even while wishing we could have an impact on a lost and dying world.

Part of that honest assessment needs to ask the question, "Has our process developed mature disciples of Christ or just church participants?" Has our means of teaching actually taught them the spiritual disciplines required to be a world changer in an ever-changing world? Christ developed followers who, through the power of the Holy Spirit, changed the world. Can we identify how we are actively changing the world for Christ today? This question of effectiveness was part of Paul's challenge to the early church and I believe it's an assessment we need to ask today.

Healthy churches learn to ask tough questions and respond to the answers they obtain. Healthy churches develop a pattern of seeking the leading of the Holy Spirit, debriefing how well they're doing in the process, and responding to the lessons they learn during the debriefing process. There are many tools that have been developed to aid church leaders through this process. I've found that it doesn't really matter which of the tools church leaders use, but that the most important thing is that leadership is open to using a tool to gather information, willing to process that information in an honest way, and then prayerfully respond to what they learn through the process.

I believe that some of the biggest questions before church leaders today are:

- Has our model of church attendance developed mature disciples of Christ?
- What do mature disciples of Christ look like?
- How can we make an assessment of maturity?
- What changes do we need to make in our structure that will better develop spiritual maturity?

Rather than focus on a long-term discipleship model, I propose that it's time for us to consider incorporating a discipleship model that is far more short-term in scope. If you find this to be an intriguing proposition… then read on!

What Does a Disciple Need to Know?

Once we have agreed to align our lives and ministries to the goal of making mature disciples of Jesus Christ the next question that comes to mind is "What does a disciple of Jesus Christ need to know in order to bring about maturity in faith?" There are hundreds of different topics that we could draw out of Scripture, dozens of books of the Bible to study, and millions of books that we could read about the application of biblical truths in our modern culture. You can find dozens and dozens of "discipleship resources" that will guide you on your journey. Where to start?

I've never been a guy to buy into turn-key discipleship programs. I don't think that any two disciples of Jesus Christ look identical. While I agree that there are key components to being a disciple of Christ, I also believe that our likes, interests, talents, abilities, and spiritual gifting will cause large areas of our discipleship to be different from those around us. I have friends in ministry who do things radically differently than I – yet I can clearly see that we're both making disciples of Jesus.

I like to think outside of the box when it comes to discipleship curriculum. I also like to seek the guidance of the Holy Spirit as I strive to disciple each person on an individual basis. I prepare for large group discipleship (sermons, Sunday school lessons, and small groups) based on the Holy Spirit's leading – trying to put my finger on the spiritual pulse of the group that I'm discipling. I approach my one-on-one discipleship time much differently. I don't think that everyone should be discipled the same way, learn the same material, and put it into practice the same way. This fluid approach is one of the things that makes one-on-one discipleship so exciting for me – it's always a new journey for both mentor and student!

Still, there are some definite spiritual disciplines that every disciple of Jesus Christ needs to develop. A disciple has to learn to read Scripture, pray, share their faith, etc. But how they learn these things, how long it takes, and what the practical application in their lives looks like isn't up to me. It's really up to the Holy Spirit. Rather than tell them what this looks like in their lives, I'd much rather guide them as they seek to hear the Holy Spirit define these things in their own personal context as He reveals His own unique purposes for their lives.

Just Six Things

This where I have to introduce you to a discussion that I had with a friend of mine named Jeff Miller. Jeff was serving as the district superintendent of the Central district of the Christian and Missionary Alliance at the time – yeah, he was my boss. He wrecked my idea of what a disciple of Christ should be taught by presenting me with the following scenario:

> "Let's say that you just led someone to the Lord. Now you have six days to disciple him or her. On each of those days you can only teach them one thing. After they have been discipled by you they will never be taught by anyone else for the rest of their lives. What six things are you going to teach them so they will become mature in their faith and effective in service?"

Wow! That is a great question! It really flies in the face of the long-term discipleship model! If I only have six days, and I can only teach six things, then I cannot depend on my preaching and teaching schedule! Especially if I'm planning on taking 30 years to preach through the Bible!

Is it really possible for me to develop a disciple of Jesus Christ by only teaching six things? I mean, didn't Jesus teach His disciples more than just six things? If He taught more than six things, then why are you limiting me to just six things?

As I think of all that Jesus did with and taught to His disciples I know I can list more than six things! Let's see...

1. How to pray with the Father.
2. How to heal the blind, the lame, those with leprosy.
3. How to speak in public.
4. How to feed the hungry.
5. How to answer questions people have.
6. How to stand face to face with opposition.
7. How to read and interpret Scripture.
8. How to teach in the Synagogue.
9. How to teach through the use of parables.
10. How to make the wind the waves disappear.
11. How to resist Satan.
12. How to follow the will of the Father.
13. Who the Holy Spirit is and how He interacts with us.
14. What it means to build into the Kingdom of God.
15. How to allow the leading of the Holy Spirit in our lives.
16. And SO MANY OTHERS!

See. I listed more than double the amount of things that Christ taught His disciples than I'm allowed in this scenario. I know there are more. If we assume that Christ was very intentional in His lesson plans with His disciples, and He taught His disciples all these things, how can I possibly get by with less? Doesn't it take years' worth of sermons, Sunday school lessons, small groups, Bible studies, prayer, and spiritual conversations, to understand these things?

Church on Sunday morning isn't enough on its own and it certainly can't simply be replaced by one-on-one discipleship relationships. We need both. Plus we need Sunday school classes, small groups, Bible studies, times of prayer, missional outreach to our friends, neighbors, and communities, mission trips, etc. There must be a way we can combine the church experience and offerings with time spent one-on-one with a spiritual mentor.

It's not possible for one person to teach another everything they need to know about God. It's not even possible for anyone to know everything there is to know about God or everything that someone needs to know about God! Only God knows that and only God can do that! In fact, one of the signs that you're on the right path of discipleship is coming to an understanding that we have only a little part to play in the process. We have to give the majority of the process to the working of the Holy Spirit. We have to realize that He is using us as a tool in His hands to complete His process in the lives of everyone around us, and our role is to simply submit ourselves to play the part He has for us to play.

While I admit that there are ***SO MANY THINGS*** that I desire to teach a disciple of Jesus Christ, I was forced to work within this six-day scenario. Let's work with the parameters of this scenario together. We need to determine which six things we think are ***the most important things*** for a disciple of Christ to know and experience so that they will become mature disciples of Christ who are effective in service.

I recommend you write your things in pencil or that you take a piece of paper and make a numbered list: 1 through 6. What are your six things?

1.
2.
3.
4.
5.
6.

I'm serious. Write down six things. Don't continue until you've thought this through. Perhaps you need to spend a bit of time in prayer. Don't rush past this. It's important. Write down your six things.

Only Six Things?

How hard was this exercise for you? This may have been the first time you've had to think through something like this. If you're like others I've brought through this journey, you found yourselves mentally going through all the stories you've read in Scripture, sermons you've heard preached, Sunday school classes you've attended, books you've read about God, personal discipleship traits you've developed and you sorted through a lot more than six things that you could have written down. You've labored over the process to determine which six things were at the top of your list, and what things could drop in importance. You wrote things down, crossed them out, thought things through, found that certain things are covered under a general heading, and finally discovered that there are, in fact, six things that make their way to the top of your list.

Or perhaps you can't quite come up with six. That's okay. I hope you came up with at least four. That's enough for now. Move on and see how the Lord moves in your heart as you continue to read. It's okay to go back to your list as you read. You may want to cross some things out, add more to the list, or move things around as you try to determine what spiritual disciplines should be top in the life of a disciple of Jesus Christ.

As I brought the leadership team at a church I was leading through this process we saw that most people had listed common things, but everyone had something on their list that others hadn't thought of. Each of the things listed represented aspects of being a disciple of Christ that had meant a great deal to their own personal discipleship process. We remembered the times when someone else taught us spiritual disciplines, discipleship aspects, or helped us discover spiritual gifts and the impact those lessons had on our own relationship with Christ and that then fueled our desire to impart that same knowledge into the lives of those we were discipling.

Some decided that it was too hard to come up with just six things so they came up with general categories and then listed some of the things that they would cover in each of those categories. I think this is a fair way to process through this question.

The Most Important Thing

Ultimately, ***what*** you end up with on your list isn't the important thing. The important thing is that you work through the thought process of determining what you would teach someone if you only had a short time to disciple them. This exercise begins to break up the misnomer that you have an entire lifetime to make a disciple. It helps us see that we need more than just church attendance to develop the spiritual disciplines required to be a mature disciple of Jesus Christ. It helps us develop a priority list and see the interconnectivity between spiritual disciplines. Then we're able to begin to develop a process by which we can teach these things to those we're discipling.

My List

This kind of a question wasn't new to me. As I served as a youth pastor our leadership team wrestled with the question, "What does a disciple of Jesus Christ look like?" Particularly, what spiritual disciplines are required in a teenage follower of Christ? Then we talked about what kinds of topics we had to cover in our teaching times, specific ministry options, and personal relationships were required to develop these spiritual disciplines in the lives of our students. As our discussions on this topic continued, we continually revised our list and made amendments to our programs. This question caused us to develop a leadership training program to help our leaders, both current and future, learn how to strategically, intentionally foster these spiritual disciplines in the lives of our students.

When this intellectual exercise was first presented to me by Jeff Miller, I referenced the mental notes I had of those many conversations and quickly came up with the following list:

1. How to read and study the Bible.
2. How to pray.
3. How to discover their spiritual gifts and use them.
4. The importance of being part of a church.
5. How to hear the voice of God speaking in their lives.
6. How to share their faith/replicate their relationship with Christ.

A friend of mine commented that most people mention knowledge-based concepts. He came at the exercise from a different approach. His six things were:

1. Intimacy with Jesus.
2. How to read and study the Bible.
3. Sanctification – understanding how to be conformed into the image of Christ.
4. How to submit ourselves to being empowered to serve through the Holy Spirit.
5. Passionate heart for taking the Gospel message to everyone.
6. How to make other disciples.

Perhaps your list incorporates many of these things too. Maybe you've already been tempted to go back to your list and update it with some of the things that we've written. That's okay, I think that our lists will change over time as we see the fruit of the concepts we're teaching as we actually implement a plan to teach others how to develop the attributes we listed. I've also found that the list is adjusted each time I begin to disciple someone in a one-on-one discipleship relationship based on the spiritual needs and interests of the person I'm meeting with. Our students may already have a good working knowledge of one or two things our list and we're able to see that there are other areas they're interested in developing that we didn't have on our list. We have to be fluid in our thinking if we're truly being led by the Holy Spirit.

After spending a few years teaching these concepts to others, and the many conversations that have followed, I've rewritten my list a few times. These rewrites have all worked off of each other, flowed into one another, and have boiled down to core principles. I'm now convinced that there is only one thing that I need instill in the heart of any disciple of Jesus Christ, whether they are new in Christ or have been part of His family for years.

If I was to disciple someone under this scenario I would teach someone how to hear and discern the voice of God – and I would take all six days to help them understand how to do this.

That's right. You heard me correctly. I would teach one and only one thing, and I would take all six days to do it. I would teach them how to hear and discern the voice of God. I think it's that important!

I believe it is crucial to teach all believers how to hear and discern the voice of God as they read Scripture, as they engage in listening prayer, to hear His voice through circumstances in their lives, as God revealed Himself through nature, in spiritual conversations with people, by reading books about God, through sermons, Sunday school classes, and small groups, by serving others, through musical worship, by meeting with mentors in life, etc. This becomes a matter of trust for the person doing the discipling – trusting that the Holy Spirit will teach them everything He wants to say in their life, rather than thinking that we have to be the one who teaches them all things.

We all know the adage that illuminates the difference between giving a person a fish that will feed them for a meal verses teaching them how to fish, which will feed them for life. By teaching someone how to hear and discern the voice of God you're allowing them to grow in their discipleship of Christ for their entire life. In fact, by learning how to hear and discern the voice of the Holy Spirit, you're putting them into the hands of the very best teacher! He knows all things. He can do all things. He desires good for us. We can certainly trust that the Holy Spirit will take good care of the person we are discipling.

This does not mean that you have to scrap your list and replace it with "Learn to hear, discern, and respond to the voice of the Holy Spirit." No, work out your list on your own. Develop it, amend it, and improve it as you meet to disciple others, learn from the process, and prayerfully hear the leading of the Holy Spirit in your own life and ministry.

Study Questions
Chapter 4
How Long Does it Take to Make Disciples?

1. How long have you been in the church?
2. How far do you think you've progressed through the spiritual formation model that is presented by your church?
3. If "starting new relationships for the purpose of bringing the Gospel into their lives" is the end-game goal of being a disciple of Christ, how well do you think that the spiritual formation model you've experienced has prepared you for that goal?
4. Have you ever been part of a ministry team that wrestled with the question "what does a disciple need to know?" Tell of your experience and the lessons you learned.

Now it's time for you to list your six things!

1.
2.
3.
4.
5.
6.

If you studying this with a group, share your six things and give a rationale for why you selected those six things.

5. How hard was it for you to come up with your six things? If you had too many, by what process did you whittle your list down to just six things.

6. What do you think of PJ's "one thing" on his list?

CHAPTER 5

HOW TO HEAR THE VOICE OF GOD IN YOUR LIFE

"And he came to the disciples
and found them sleeping.
And he said to Peter,
"So, could you not watch with me one hour?
Watch and pray that you may not
enter into temptation.
The spirit indeed is willing, but the flesh is weak."
Matthew 26:40-41.

Learning to hear the voice of God is crucial if we want to live our lives missionally and become a fully-devoted, mature disciple of Jesus Christ. There is a big difference between doing what we think God wants us to do and going with the Lord, following His leading, asking Him to work in us and then through us. The first leads us to very limited results. We might look busy, we might be doing a lot of "Christian" things at church, but we're not being conformed into His image by developing into a mature disciple who makes more mature disciples – which is a natural result of hearing His voice and allowing Him to work in us and then through us.

This really is the difference between working ***for Christ*** and working ***with Christ***? How do we really know the difference? Missional living begins with listening prayer and doesn't take another step until we hear His voice in prayer. Then we confirm what we're hearing to ensure that we're hearing from Him. Then we take a step of obedience, following Christ's leading, and we pause and confirm that we're going with Him, listen to His leading for our next step, and then we repeat the process over and over and over again.

Jesus usually only gives us one step at a time. David understood this as he wrote Psalm 119. Verse 105 is one that is probably familiar to you: "Your word is a lamp to my feet and a light to my path." God's word (His Written Word, His Spoken Word, the Inspired Word, etc.) is a lamp to my feet. It just lights where my feet need to go. It doesn't light the whole way at once. It doesn't light the things that I don't need to see. It goes with me. It shows me what I need to see right now – today! It's a light to my path – it clearly shows me the way the Lord wants me to go. When I learn to use God's Word as a light to my path I realize that I will never be lead astray! It always shows me my next step. There are many times I would like to know the big picture, see more than just the next step, or know where in the world this path ends up – but God only shows me the next step. I can trust that He also knows the step after that, the step after that, and the step after that, etc. etc.

This concept of being able to hear the voice of God may be a new one for you. Most of our culture believes that anyone who says they're hearing God tell them to do something needs to have their head examined, but Scripture is full of stories of men and women who believed that God was communicating with them in a personal, intimate way – and a major theme found throughout Scripture is that the living God is a speaking God.

In his book, *The Pursuit of God*, A.W. Tozer put it this way:

> "An intelligent plain man, untaught in the truths of Christianity, coming upon this text [the Book of John], would likely conclude that John meant to teach that it is the nature of God to speak, to communicate His thoughts to others. And he would be right. A word is a medium by which thoughts are expressed, and the application of term to the Eternal Son leads us to believe that self-expression is inherent in the Godhead, that God is forever seeking to speak Himself out to His creation. The whole Bible supports the idea. God is speaking. Not God spoke, but God is speaking. He is by His nature continuously articulate. He fills the world with His speaking Voice." (Tozer, p.53)

I did not realize that I could personally hear the voice of God speaking in my life until I was in my late 30s. Throughout my life I knew that God was speaking to me, and I knew I was hearing His voice, but it took me a while to learn to properly recognize His voice and intently listen to what He had to say to me. Although I had been in church all of my life, listened to hundreds of sermons, regularly read Scripture, spent time in personal worship, read books about God, spent times in prayer, and had many spiritual conversations with spiritual mentors, I did not realize that I could intently hear the voice of God in my life until I went on a mission trip with a group of students I was pastoring. It wasn't until then that I realized exactly how God was speaking His truth into my life, how I should interpret that truth, and how I was supposed to apply it to my daily life.

God Speaks in a Variety of Ways

There is no end to the ways that God speaks to us. Scripture is a good place for us to start to hear the voice of God in our lives. We know that it is the Written Word of God (2 Timothy 3:16 & 2 Peter 1:21). There are dozens of other ways that God speaks to us. Consider the following ways Scripture mentions that God speaks to us:

- Through His creation. (Romans 1:20.)
- In visions. (Revelation 1.)
- As we sleep through dreams. (Job 33:15.)
- In a miraculous burning bush. (Exodus 3:2.)
- Both through what His Prophets spoke and wrote. (Hebrews 1:1.)
- Communicated through angels. (Luke 1:26.)
- Testing through a fleece. (Judges 6:36-40.)
- In listening prayer. (Romans 8:26-27.)
- Through His still, small voice. (1 Kings 19:12.)
- Demonstrated through miraculous events. (Exodus 7-11.)
- In the life, teachings, and miracles of Jesus. (The entirety of the Gospels.)
- By writing on the wall. (Daniel 5:5.)
- In every way through the ministry of the Holy Spirit. (John 14.)
- Through time spent with Christian mentors. (Titus 2.)
- Through the preaching of His Word. (Jonah 3 & Acts 7.)
- In worship. (2 Chronicles 20.)
- By casting lots. (Acts 1:23-26.)
- Even through a donkey. (Numbers 22:28.)

While there are no limits as to how God speaks to us, there are a few good places for us to position ourselves to learn to better hear His voice. We can learn to hear His voice clearly through reading Scripture, times of worship, engaging in listening prayer, listening to sermons, reading books such as this one, having conversations with spiritual mentors, by serving others, asking Him to speak through visions and dreams, and through circumstances that we experience each day. The Holy Spirit uses each of these means to communicate His will for our lives. As we learn to hear His voice we can hear what He is saying to us each and every day.

Visions and Dreams

After hearing an Alliance missionary talk about the number of people coming to know Christ on the mission field through visions and dreams, I began to ask the Lord to speak through visions and dreams for myself, my family, and those I minister to. Many of these stories involved Jesus Christ coming to people in visions and dreams to call them unto Himself. Then, the missionary only had to explain the Gospel Message and the person was ready to commit their life to Christ. When this happens one time we're amazed at how the Lord reveals Himself for His glory. When this happens on a regular basis, it is easy to see that God is actively at work in the lives of those around us.

Not everyone is going to hear the voice of the Lord speaking in their lives in the same way. While the general revelation of His creation, and His Written Word, will speak to everyone, He may choose to speak to you in all or none of the additional means listed above. The important thing is that you are able to hear Him speak to you – not how He speaks to you!

Since asking Jesus to speak through visions and dreams I actively look for Him to speak this way. As I outline below, we always have to test what we believe we are hearing from Him. Not every idea that comes into my head is an idea from Him – not every dream I remember when I wake up in the morning is from Him, but some are. When we learn how to hear Him as He speaks to us through any of the means above, we have greater confidence that He's actively working in our lives every day!

Our Posture is Key

The degree to which we are able to hear His voice speaking in our lives has a lot to do with our approach and attitude as we strive to position ourselves to hear Him. Am I reading the Bible so that I can "put my time in with God" or so that I can hear His voice? Am I spending time in prayer so that I can leave my "to do list" with God or so that I can hear His voice? Am I attending church so that I look like a good Christian or am I expecting Him to speak to me through worship, the Sunday school lesson, and the sermon? Am I just hoping He'll answer the emotional need I feel at this particular moment, or am I expecting Him to tell me how He is going to use me to help meet the needs of others? Do I pick up books about Jesus because they're going to tell me what I want to hear, or am I reading books that will stretch my understanding of Him and challenge my level of obedience to Him? Do I have conversations with Christian mentors and friends so that I can unload the junk in my life, ask them to tell me what I want to hear, and gossip about others – or so that I can gain godly advice, so that we can encourage, learn from, and pray for each other?

How to Get Started

If you're new at trying to hear the voice of God, then here is a simple, eight-step process to learn to hear the voice of God in your life through listening prayer. The process is simple, but if this is a new concept of prayer for you, it might take some practice before you're able to clearly hear His voice. If this doesn't come easily to you, don't give up! This is a crucial spiritual discipline to develop and it will be worth the investment. Any new skill, habit, or discipline takes time to develop.

1. **Prepare to pray**. Turn off all of your distraction devices. Set 60 minutes aside. Find a quiet place where you won't be interrupted.

2. **Worship**. Put your headphones on and spend about 20 minutes worshipping Him with some worship music of your

choice. Worship music prepares your heart to hear from the Lord. There is a reason why the worship service at your church has worship music before the sermon!

3. **Pray**. Use whatever prayer method you choose. My favorite is Power Praying by David Chotka. Be sure to ask the Lord to search your heart to identify sin in your life, confess that sin, repent of it, and ask Him to prepare your heart to hear His voice. Unconfessed sin is always a barrier to hearing God speak to us. We must deal with our sin before we hear His assignments for the day.

4. **Be still and listen**. This is the hardest for most of us. Try to spend 15 minutes still before Him, simply listening to what He is saying to you. If you're like me, your mind is going to wander as you learn to be still and listen. As your mind wanders, check to see if it's God speaking to you. Ask Him to clarify. If your mind is wandering down a path that is not from the Lord, learn the discipline of bringing your mind back to asking Him to speak to you. As you hear Him speak you should write down what you're hearing. Then you can test it later.

5. **Ask a question**. While you're still before Him, ask Him a specific question and wait for His answer. I've found that I often ask Him the wrong questions. If I'm not getting clear direction I change the question I'm asking Him or ask Him to give me the question I should be asking. You can never go wrong asking Him questions like, "What is Your will in this situation?" or "How can You use me to expand Your Kingdom in my life and in the lives around me?" or "What sin is separating me from You today?"

6. **Read His Written Word**. Ask Him to bring you to a passage that will speak directly into your life.

7. **Test what you're hearing**. Testing is a crucial step to ensure that what you're hearing is really coming from the Lord. Many times we can mistake the will of the Lord for our own thoughts or desires. See the section on testing below.

8. **Thank Him for speaking to you**. Now you can move forward in your day with confidence, knowing that He's continuing to speak to you.

As you become more practiced in listening prayer you will better be able to hear the voice of the Lord speaking in your life. You will learn to be able to just "reset your thinking" to be able to hear Him clearly with little effort. Just as if you're learning to know the voice of a close friend, you will learn to hear God's voice as well. When you know the Lord is always speaking to you, and when you learn to hear His voice speak specifically into your life, you will become more and more excited to spend time with Him to hear what He's saying. Then we can move forward in our lives with confidence, knowing that we're following His leading and that He is with us as we move forward.

Some people have asked me if there is a shorter way to spend time with the Lord – like just 5, 10, or 15 minutes instead of the hour I suggest. All I can say is that the amount of spiritual benefit you will get out of your time with the Lord is usually directly proportional to the amount of time you put into it. There are no shortcuts in developing relationships. You're not going to be a close friend with someone you give 5, 10, or 15 minutes to each day. You have to spend more time with them in order to know them intimately. It is the same with your relationship with the Lord.

I often turn to the account of Jesus and His disciples in the Garden of Gethsemane when I'm asked how long we need to pray. Jesus asked His disciples to join Him in prayer as He prepared to offer Himself as the sacrifice for the sins of the world. There are other times where Jesus went off into a quiet place to pray on His own for hours – or through the entire night, but this time He only asks His disciples for an hour:

> "And he came to the disciples and found them sleeping. And he said to Peter, "So, could you not watch with me one hour? Watch and pray that you may not enter into temptation. The spirit indeed is willing, but the flesh is weak." Matthew 26:40-41.

Part of me wants to say, "If you only have 15 minutes to pray then 15 minutes is better than nothing." But that advice always comes with resignation. A larger part of me wants to say, "If you can't set an hour aside for the Lord every day or two then you need to look at how genuine your faith is and how you're spending your time!" We often give 60 minutes to our favorite TV show, 120 minutes to a movie, and 3 or 4 hours to a sporting event. Do we really think those are more important than spending time with Jesus Christ?

You Must Test It!

As you dwell in the Lord's presence, you're going to hear one of four voices speak to you. The first is your own sinful nature (or just your own ideas), the second is Satan's voice, the third is the voice of the world (the non-stop media assault, peer pressure, and the ideas and solutions of those who don't know Christ), and the fourth is the Lord's voice. At first it might be hard to discern the differences between these four voices, but with time you can learn to quickly test what you're hearing to discern if it's truly from the Lord.

Your Own Sinful Nature

Your sinful nature promotes one, and only one thing: YOU! It says things like:

- You're the best.
- You deserve it.
- Nobody's giving you the respect you deserve.
- If you could only get the chance you've earned.

- You have to protect what you've built.
- You don't have to share.
- You don't have to give credit to others.
- You are the most important person in the world.

Satan's Voice

Satan often partners with your sinful nature and agrees with the things that you are saying to yourself. Just as we often seek others to agree with our thoughts and opinions, we search our own thoughts and sift through things to determine if we're right in our thinking or not. Satan is going to agree with our thinking until we hear a chorus of voices in our head, all saying, "You deserve this…"

The World's Opinions

I'm amazed at how many times Christians seek the world's advice for their lives; completely passing by the advice Scripture has for our lives. We turn to psychiatrists, psychologists, and counselors who are standing on the ideas of man before we prayerfully seek God's will. We turn to medicine before we turn to God for healing. We are bombarded with messages that tell us how to spend our time, our money, and our resources, yet we completely ignore God's plan for these crucial areas of our life. We get caught up in the "bigger and better" mentality that is the only hope the world has to offer. We spend our money in ways that are contrary to Scripture and then ask God why He's not providing enough for us. When we ascribe to the world's ways we will never have enough, we will never be good enough; we will never be satisfied.

The Lord's Voice

The simplest ways to know if we're hearing the Lord's voice is that His voice always exalts Himself and humbles us before Him. He is Holy. He is perfect. He alone deserves our praise. We find His will when we're willing to humble ourselves before Him, confess our sin, and allow Him to dictate the priorities of our lives!

AIM's 5-Step Testing Method

Seth Barnes is the founder and director of Adventures in Missions (AIM). He has developed a great 5-step testing method in his AIM 100 Mission Trip Training material. Learning how to apply these 5 steps will help you discern if what you're hearing is really from the Lord:

1. Does it match what you read in Scripture?
2. Do spiritual mentors affirm that it is from God?
3. Does it exalt Jesus Christ?
4. Does it produce good fruit?
5. Does Jesus Christ bring it pass?

Let's look at each of these five points a little closer.

Does it Match what You Read in Scripture?

God never gives us permission to step outside of the bounds of what we know in Scripture. He's not going to give you special permission to sin. If you're sensing God's desire for you to step outside of His Law, or other biblical directives, you can be sure that you're not hearing from the Lord.

Do Spiritual Mentors Affirm that it is From God?

As you seek the advice of other Christians, be sure that you're asking spiritual mentors for their advice rather than asking the advice of those who are weaker in their faith. Sometimes we're just seeking the affirmation of those who we know will agree with us. This isn't going to help us know what God has for us – it's only going to foster the desires of our own sinful nature, follow Satan's will for us, or adopt the patterns of the world. I know that my heart is just like Jeremiah 17:9 says: "The heart is deceitful above all things, and desperately sick; who can understand it." I know that my original bent is to go against the will of God and trend to my own desires. I need to seek the advice of spiritual mentors who are going to give me wise, biblical counsel, pray with me, and help me move in the direction the Lord wants me to go. I'm sure you do as well.

Does it Exalt Jesus Christ?

I want my life to exalt Jesus Christ! I want to lift Him up, not myself. I want others to know how Great He is, not how great I am. I want their lives to change because they met Him, not because they met me. The things that Jesus leads me to do will cause others to praise Him and be thankful for my willingness to be part of what He's doing – rather than exalt me for my wisdom, my ingenuity, my patience, etc. and thank the Lord for allowing them to be part of my ministry. Many times this difference is subtle. Spiritual mentors can help us discern the difference.

I struggle with taking the credit for the way He's working in my life and ministry. This is called pride. I want God to receive the glory for all that He's doing in my life and then through my life, but often times I elbow Him out of the place of glory and instead place it on myself. If I, or others, have to struggle to see God's hand in something, it's a good indication that I'm doing it on my own strength, I'm fulfilling my own will, and I'm going to get limited results every time. Conversely, when Jesus Christ is the one who receives the glory, the results are much more significant.

Does it Produce Good Fruit?

Does what you're hearing from the Lord bring about good fruit in your life? Is He calling you out of sin? You won't feel shame and guilt, but forgiveness and grace. Is He calling you to further steps of obedience?

He won't leave you to figure them out for yourself, but will guide you through the steps of becoming more obedient to Him. Is He telling you that you have to resolve conflict in a relationship? Jesus outlined the steps to restore relationships in Matthew 18. These are always good steps to take to resolve conflict in relationships.

Remember, God doesn't give us the whole plan at once. He gives us one step at a time – the directives for one day at a time. Don't worry about tomorrow. Just worry about following Him today. Over and over again in Scripture we see that God has tomorrow covered. We just need to focus on today. Ask a question. Hear His answer. Step out in obedience. Test the peace. Adjust as necessary. Repeat.

The peace of Christ that Paul talks about in Colossians 3:15 becomes a great tool for determining if something is from God. As you step out in obedience to His leading, do you sense His peace or do you experience anxiety? Is there confusion? Is there joy? Is there anger, resentment, or pride? These become great indications if we're following the path that God has for us or if we're out on our own. As we learn to gauge our thoughts and emotions, they help us test to see if we're walking with the Holy Spirit or striking out on our own.

Does Jesus Christ Bring it to Pass?

Ultimately we know if something is from God when He brings it to pass. God doesn't mess with our lives. He doesn't lead us down dead ends. He doesn't have to guess if something is going to work. He loves us. He wants us to trust Him because He is able to do all things. Ephesians 3:20-21 says, "Now to him who is able to do far more abundantly than all that we ask or think, according to the power at work within us, to him be glory in the church and in Christ Jesus throughout all generations, forever and ever. Amen."

Sometimes we ask the Lord to do something specific, like asking for a job, money to meet a need, to take us to another spiritual level, or a solution for a relationship conflict. If we apply the answer we think we're hearing from Him, and it leads to failure, then we didn't hear Him correctly, or we need to wait for His timing.

We may have to wait days, weeks, months, or many years to see Jesus bring something to pass! The peace of Christ becomes a great indicator for us to know if He's working – and we have to wait – or if we're asking Him to do something that is against His will. Our time with Him will give us the peace to know He's working and the patience for His timing.

Everyone Can Do It!

I once taught a group of guys how to hear the voice of the Lord at a Saturday morning men's breakfast at church. We met together for breakfast, had a time of worship, and then I introduced the topic of listening prayer. As I introduced the topic and told them that they were going to sit before the Lord to hear from Him I asked them to offer their thoughts as we began. Some of them said, "I've never done anything like this before." Others said, "I don't think I can sit quietly before the Lord for that long." One candidly said, "I don't think this is going to work." I asked them to give it a try no matter what apprehension they were experiencing. Each of them looked for some space to be alone with their Bible and pad of paper to hear from the Lord.

After the 20 minutes was up I asked them to meet together in the main room again. I was met with, "Already? Is our time up already?" One guy said, "There is no way that was 20 minutes!"

I responded, "You're right. It was actually 30 minutes. I lost track of the time we were supposed to stop praying and I ended up giving you extra time."

After we had gathered together at the tables again I asked them to share what they heard the Lord saying to them during their time of listening prayer. Every single one of them had a Bible passage to share, a memory, or an encouraging thought the Lord brought to their mind as they prayed. Some were shocked that they actually heard Him speak to them. Every one of them said they heard something they really needed to hear that day.

"God spoke personally and intimately to each and every one of us!" I pointed out. "The big question is, 'if we know that we will hear from God when we're quiet before Him, then why don't we do this every day?'" I mean, think about it. If we're not willing to sit before Him, with Bible and paper before us, then in effect we're saying to the Lord that we have more important things to do than be quiet before Him so we can hear His voice. We're saying that we're not willing to hear His will, but that we really just want Him to rubber stamp our will and make it happen for us.

I don't want to be a guy that tells my Creator I don't have time to spend with Him! I'm sure you don't either.

Barriers to Hearing the Voice of God

I think the biggest reason it's hard for us to learn how to sit quietly before the Lord is because we live in a culture that never takes a break. We wake up and head to work or school, then off to practice, shopping, or maybe another job. Media demands our attention – there's always a movie to see, TV to watch, or a sporting event that promises be to a "must-see event of the year!" Add to that our Facebook, email, text messages, as well as following rabbit trail after rabbit trail online, and you can see why it's hard for us to be quiet before Him. I can open my browser to check the weather radar and see an interesting video promoted on the side of the page. I pick on it only to see another interesting article promoted on the side of that page. I pick on it and read it. It starts my mind down a path that I just have to research right now! Then my Facebook notifications pop and I just have to give my full attention to them! An hour has gone by and now the weather radar map that I originally looked at is no longer valid, so it starts all over again!

So, you can see why it's so important to turn off all of the distractions around you when you're trying to be still before the Lord. Yes, you can turn your cell phone off!!! You will live without knowing who calls you, texts, tweets, or messages you for the next hour! You can press the "Airplane Mode" button on your computer (or shut it off), and not answer the door for 60 minutes so that you can give the Lord your full attention. Every time you let one of those things demand your attention you might have to start all over again when you go before Him.

That sin we're holding onto creates a solid barrier, keeping us from hearing the voice of the Lord. Pride, gossip, dissention, envy, abuse, addiction, sexual immorality (which is any sexual activity outside of that between one man and woman who are married to each other), greed, gluttony, coveting, as well as idolatry, and other disobedience – these sins will hinder our ability to clearly hear the voice of the Lord speaking in our lives.

Isaiah understood that this barrier extended both ways: you can't hear God speaking to you, and God is not hearing you speak to Him. It's not really that God isn't "hearing you speak to Him," as if you need to speak louder because He's too far away, but that He's not going to respond to you until you're willing to humble yourself before Him and do things His way.

> "But your iniquities have made a separation
> Between you and your God,
> And your sins have hidden his face from you
> So that he does not hear."
> Isaiah 59:2.

You simply can't be obedient to God and disobedient to God at the same time. A true disciple doesn't accept some things from the Lord and reject others. While all of us struggle against sin, we must take a posture of allowing the Holy Spirit to identify the sin and sanctify us of the sin, rather than fighting against the process or completely ignoring it. We can't choose which sin we're going to surrender to God and which sin we're going to hold onto and develop a close, personal, intimate relationship with God! God's holiness demands full obedience. If you're having a hard time hearing the voice of the Lord you should ask Him to do a heart-check to identify the sin in your life. Then, confess it, repent of it (work on going in a completely different direction), and again seek His voice.

This is an issue that has become an epidemic in the modern American church! We go to church on Sundays, we listen to the sermon while we play on our phone, we may even lead a ministry, we "try to do our best" – and we think that we're being true followers of Christ. We're really just working on being spiritual on our own strength. We're adding to our spiritual lives in one spoonful per week, rather than feasting at the abundant table He sets before us each and every day. We look better than others around us, we experience some spiritual successes, and we think that we're doing what a good Christian does, but Christ has demanded far more than this from us. He demands our full obedience. He demands that we replace our own personal will for our lives with His will for our lives.

This message isn't very popular in the modern church! It's offensive to those who want Jesus to meet their needs. We've selfishly grown to look at God as our personal divine butler, expecting Him to give us what we want, right when we want it. Some are asking for material things. Some are asking for healing. Some are asking for answers to questions. All of these can be good things to ask for, but if we don't give Him the right to decide what is best for us then we're just imposing our will on God. We demand that He does things our way and then we're very upset with Him when He doesn't respond the way we want Him to respond.

Now, I realize that most of us would never admit that we're treating God as a divine butler. Most of us are abhorred at the concept that we would demand anything of God, but if we're not willing to allow God to demand ***ANYTHING and EVERYTHING*** of us, then we're not going to be able to clearly hear His voice.

What You're NOT Going to Hear From the Lord

You are going to be disappointed if you go into your prayer time thinking that you're going to hear God speak to you in an audible voice, get an email with God's notes on your daily agenda, see a billboard with God's direction for you on your way to work, or hear Him give you everything you need for the rest of your life. Sometimes God does speak this way, but most often He just gives us the next step for our day. God speaks in an audible voice as we're in a conversation with someone and we hear God's will for us. He will speak through our emails, but it will be through someone else writing to us. We'll be listening to the radio and hear something that God is speaking directly to our hearts in a song or something the DJ has to say. We'll open our Bibles to read something that was written 2,000 years ago, but it seems as if it was written just for us, today.

God usually reveals His will to us in the short term only. There are times He will say something that will be a promise to us for the rest of our lives, but mostly God tells us what we need to hear today. Why does He do this? It's because He wants to develop our relationship with Him and our faith in Him. This is done as we talk with Him each day and trust what He's saying to us. Plus, most of us are lazy procrastinators. Our first inclination is to only go to God to take care of all the tough stuff we can't handle on our own and we often wait until the very last minute before we go to Him.

"God fix this! I've got an emergency. I need your help now!"

Nobody likes to be the person people call only when they need something "Right now!" While there are in fact things that come up suddenly, I've learned that most "emergencies" in my life are in fact situations that have been building for a very long time. I'm heading off the emergencies long before they become an urgent issue that will cause irreparable harm by spending time with the Lord every day, by hearing what He's telling me every day, and by following His will for my life every day.

God Decides What He's Going to Say to Us

What does God say during the time I spend in listening prayer? Exactly what I need to hear that day. At times, He brings me to a Bible passage that I need to be reminded of. Another time He brings a worship song to mind that affirms something that I need to worship Him for. Almost every time, He draws me in close and reminds me of His love again. I always ask Him to point out sin in my life and confess it to Him. Near the end of my time of prayer I always hear Him call me to a deeper walk with Him. Quite often, He gives me assignments for me to join Him in the work He's doing. He will lead me to a person to pray for, prompt me to send an encouraging note, lead me to a person who is seeking answers, and I can always follow His leading with an expectation that something good is going to come of it.

Ultimately, I go into sessions of listening prayer expecting the Holy Spirit to speak to me. I leave how He speaks to me up to Him, and I leave what He says to me up to Him.

Long Sessions Prepare Us To Hear "On the Fly"

The time we spend in our quiet, dwelling, determined times of listening prayer prepare us to better hear the voice of the Holy Spirit speaking as we go about our day. God isn't going to give us everything we need to know about our day in one download. He's going to give us a general direction to head in our day and then guide us one step at a time.

In Christ's divinity He knows all things about all people at all times, but He set His divinity aside while He was on earth as a man. He would have also set aside His knowledge of all people alive at that time. That is why He prayed often to hear the will of the Father

(Luke 5:16), and work in the power of the Holy Spirit (Acts 10:38). I'm sure He was also demonstrating these two important things for us, as well.

His regular time in prayer with the Father prepared Him to hear the Father's will as He went about His day. In John 5 we read the account of Jesus healing a man who was lying by the Pool of Bethesda. As He and His disciples approached the man, the Holy Spirit must have revealed to Him that this man had been by the pool for a long time. Jesus did not ask the man if he had been there for quite some time. He didn't say, "How long have you been by this pool?" Nor did He ascertain that he must have been there for quite some time because of the man's surroundings. He didn't say, "It appears to me that you have been sitting here for quite some time..." No, Jesus was in tune with the voice of the Father speaking through the Holy Spirit, and He knew how to best minister to this man. Jesus said to him, "Do you want to be healed?"

We too can "tune in" to the will of the Father through the prompting of the Holy Spirit as we spend extended times in prayer and then listen for His leading throughout our days.

Real-Life Example

I was helping a college student look at a number of summer employment options. She was given a recommendation for a potential position from a source at school, but that option would take her away from the support structure she had through family, Christian friends, at her church, and it would probably put her into an unhealthy partying environment. Was the Lord calling her to go there to be a witness for Him? Or would the pull to be part of the partying crowd be too great for her? She wanted to hear what the Lord had planned for her. We dedicated some time each day for one week to pray and ask the Lord to speak to us specifically regarding what she should do. We didn't even have to pray for the entire week before she was sure of what the Lord wanted her to do.

As we met together to test what she was hearing, we determined that the option that took her into a partying crowd:

- Didn't match Scriptural directives to live a holy lifestyle.
- Her mentors didn't think she was strong enough to stand against the temptation on her own – apart from her family, her church, and her Christian friends.
- Jesus would not be exalted if she fell to temptation.
- While there was the potential for her to see good fruit as she witnessed to others through the position, the pull do the wrong things might eradicate that potential.
- As soon as she asked Jesus for His input, He started to close the doors to the opportunity and began to open the doors to another, better opportunity for her.

As soon as she said, "No!" to the first opportunity, He led her to an opportunity that:

- Allowed her to live a holy lifestyle, including blessing others through her help.
- Through prayer and fasting, her spiritual mentors affirmed that this would be a good opportunity for her.
- Jesus was exalted as she had many spiritual conversations with the group she worked with.
- The good fruit was found in holy living, being a big help, and the further development of healthy relationships.
- Looking back on the decision, it was clear to see that this is what He had for her to do with her summer.

This is Missional Living

As we learn to sit before the Lord to hear His voice in our lives we are developing one of the key spiritual disciplines required to live our lives missionally. Listening prayer will take practice – both to learn how to hear His voice better, and then to hear Him as we go about our day. Ultimately, when we're able to clearly hear the prompting of the Holy Spirit, and quickly learn to test if what we're hearing is from Him, we'll be able to step out with full confidence and live our lives missionally each and every day.

Check out my book entitled, *Mission Possible: Living the Great Commission* for an easy to follow, six-step missional living plan that will help you live your life missionally each and every day.

Study Questions
Chapter 5
How to Hear the Voice of God in Your Life?

1. How familiar are you with the concept of listening prayer?

2. How do you hear the voice of God speaking in your life?

3. Has God spoken to you in visions and dreams? If so, tell a story of a time He did.

4. Are there other ways that God has spoken to you in your life? How so?

Spend at least one session in listening prayer. Then answer the following questions:

5. How hard was it for you to set this hour aside?

6. How hard was it for you to sit still before the Lord?

7. What did you hear the Lord say to you during your time of prayer?

8. Test what you heard from the Lord!

    - Does it match what you read in Scripture?
    - Do spiritual mentors affirm that it is from God?
    - Does it exalt Jesus Christ?
    - Does it produce good fruit?
    - Does Jesus Christ bring it pass?

9. What barriers to hearing the Voice of God have you identified in your life?

10. What can you do to free up more time to spend in listening prayer on a regular basis?

CHAPTER 6

AN AMAZING GROWTH STRATEGY

"And let us consider how to stir up one another to love and good works, not neglecting to meet together, as is the habit of some, but encouraging one another, and all the more as you see the Day drawing near." Hebrews 10:24-25.

In Chapter 1 we discussed the difference between a convert to Christianity and being a disciple of Jesus Christ. We said that a convert is someone who has made a decision to accept Jesus Christ's sacrifice on the cross, to ask Jesus Christ into their life to be their personal savior, to forgive them of their sins, to bring them from an eternity separated from God to an eternity with God in heaven when they die. Usually a convert does this by raising a hand in a public gathering, by coming forward to an altar at the front of a church, by saying the sinner's prayer, by responding to a call given by a preacher, or by reading a tract or a book.

Let's use the definition of a disciple that I offered at the beginning of this book:

> A disciple is ***a student of Jesus Christ***, who is submitting themselves to being transformed into the image of Jesus Christ, through the experience of relationship, through the development of biblical knowledge, and effective service as part of the body of Christ.

Now let's set up a scenario where you are able to convert someone to Christianity through a short encounter at some point in your day. This could be a stranger on a street corner, someone you work with, someone you run into at Wal-Mart, or someone you're waiting in line behind at the bank. This could be a stranger that you've never met before or a friend that you're having a conversation with. In this short encounter, you're able to convince this person that they need to pray the sinner's prayer; they then pray the prayer, and you each go on your own way. You may or may not ever see them again.

For the purposes of this discussion, let's say that you are able to convert one person each day for 34 years. At the end of 34 years you will have converted just over 12,000 people. Wahoo! Most of you who are reading this may be thinking, "Wouldn't it be great if I was able to do that!"

Under this scenario these people are set free to live their lives without even understanding the "decision" they just made. They don't know what it really means to give their lives to Christ and walk with Him throughout their lives. You may have done nothing more than simply convince them to pray a prayer. Some of them may have acquiesced to your request out of respect for your friendship, out of sheer politeness, or out of a desire to end the conversation with you as quickly as possible! They might have been thinking, "All right, I'll pray the prayer if you'll just leave me alone."

Now, working off our definition of discipleship, let's say that we've developed a process where it takes us one year for us to intentionally make a true disciple of Jesus Christ. During this time we develop a relationship with someone and help them understand their need to develop their own personal relationship with Jesus Christ. Then, after they give their lives to Him, we teach them how to hear and discern the voice of the Lord in their life through His Written Word, through prayer, sermons, books about God, circumstances, worship, etc. We teach them how to identify their spiritual gifts, the importance of using them in an active, healthy body of believers, and we ensure they're well on their way to develop a mature relationship with Christ and are effective servants who build into His Kingdom.

At the end of the year we say, "Now, go do likewise." Now the two of us pray about who God would have us disciple next. God opens our eyes to two more that we can develop relationship with, show Jesus to, and then lead into a discipleship relationship with Christ. At the end of the second year, we say, "Now, go do likewise."

And so on, and so on, etc. etc.

At the end of that same 34 year period we have discipled over 8 billion people. ***Yeah, 8 billion people!*** Right now, as I write this, there are an estimated 7,290,701,855 people alive (according to the US Census Bureau). 322,295,795 of those live in the United States of America.

Jesus didn't send us to convert people to a religious thought process, to get them to pray the "sinner's prayer," or to get them to respond to an emotionally-charged message. Jesus said that we are to make disciples. He commands this in a passage called "The Great Commission."

> "And Jesus came and said to them, "All authority in heaven and on earth has been given to me. Go therefore

and make disciples of all nations, baptizing them in the name of the Father and of the Son and of the Holy Spirit, teaching them to observe all that I have commanded you. And behold, I am with you always, to the end of the age." Matthew 28:18-20.

Think of the Growth!

The example of 8 billion people discipled I outlined above is based on the concept of one person who is living their life making disciples who are then making more disciples. Think of how much faster we could make disciples if the entire church would all take part?!?! In fact, if this year just 10 people took this challenge seriously, and began to disciple one person for a year, who then in turn discipled others, etc. The 8 billion mark would be reached in just over 30 years. If 100 people took the challenge we would reach 8 billion in just over 27 years. If 1,000 people took the challenge we would reach 8 billion in just over 23 years. The return on the growth starts small at first (one a year), but it doesn't take long for us to see a HUGE return on our investment in 5, 10, 20, or 30 years.

Dream with me! The US Census Bureau says there are about 314 million people in America. We could evangelize and disciple the entire US in about 15 years if we took Christ's words to make disciples seriously and implemented an intentional plan to disciple others one-on-one. Discipleship is how we can really pass a better world onto the next generations.

Why Aren't We Done Yet?

I know that there are many Christians who are following healthy discipleship models today. I know that I'm not the only one who is using a healthy pattern of discipleship in life, the only pastor who talks about this, or the only author who has postulated these concepts. I know that there are many healthy churches who are effectively reaching their communities with the life-giving message of the Gospel.

I know there are many people who have previously understood what it is to be a convert who are getting on board with becoming a mature disciple of Jesus Christ and then making more disciples of Christ.

Yet most studies show that church growth isn't keeping up with population numbers. Many times what we see as church growth is really just new people moving into town or people changing churches. In both cases, some other church's attendance numbers went down in order for your church numbers to go up. Healthy church growth is based on conversion growth. Those are people who didn't attend church, who didn't know Christ, but have found Him and are now attending church. Many churches have seen little or no conversions or baptisms in years. In fact, I've seen a statistical category that reported the number of churches who have not seen ANY conversions or baptisms in more than a decade. A decade! What are we doing as a church?!?!

We simply need to do a better job of making disciples who make disciples!

But the very fact of the matter is that most people who call themselves Christians are not making disciples. They're not even making converts. They're not even bringing new people into church with them. And I don't understand why!

I like to challenge those I lead to consider what church would look like if everyone brought just one new person into the church every year. Just one new person per year. That's not one new person per week, or one new person per month – just one new person per year. Our church would more than double in size each and every year. This is such a simple church growth strategy! Every church could use it. If each and every one of us knows about 150 people, even considering that 50 of those people are people we know at church already, we still know 100 people who we can invite to come to church with us. We just need to see one of them come to church a year. That certainly sounds feasible to me!

Let me bring this closer to home. Ready to feel uncomfortable? Ask yourself the following questions:

- How many people have you brought into your church this year?
- By what process did you bring them into your church?
- Why didn't you bring more people into the church?
- How many people did you invite to come to church with you this year?
- What's keeping you from inviting the 100 people around you each and every day to church with you this week? If they don't come this week – then you need to invite them again next week, and the next week, and the next week!

For some of us we have to ask the question, "How many years has it been since we brought ***one new person*** to church with us?"

Whose Job Is It?

Many people add the task of "growing the church" to the pastor's job description. In addition to preaching and teaching each Sunday, leading prayer meetings, leading a small group, developing leadership in the church, counseling with families in the church, visiting people in the hospital and the nursing home, checking in with those who missed church this week, introducing yourself to the new people at church this week, being available for those emergencies that invariably pop up each week; pastors are expected to meet new people in town, develop relationships with them, invite them to church, and then disciple them once they are part of the church. Sure, pastors should do most of these things, but if you think that pastors are the only persons in a church who are to grow it, then you've got to adjust your view of outreach!

The easiest way to determine how much your view of outreach needs to be adjusted is by asking yourself the simple question, "How many people have I brought into the church this year?"

Even if the pastor was able to bring one new person in the church each week (which I think is a ***very*** ambitious goal!) he still cannot outpace the growth that would occur when everyone in the church brought one new person in the church per year! (Assuming that there are more than 50 people in the church.)

Brought In or Prayed In

In my experience people are integrated into a church in one of two ways:

1. They are brought in by those who are already part of the church.
2. They are prayed in by those who are already part of the church.

I'm okay with either approach. In fact, I prefer that ***both approaches*** exist in a ministry I lead, but most churches will experience growth if church leadership is willing to fully invest itself in planning, training, and implementing just one of these approaches.

Studies have shown that most unchurched people would attend church if they were genuinely asked to come to an appropriate event by someone they already know. Most of them won't come because they heard the advertisement on the radio, saw the poster at Wal-Mart, had a stranger knock on their door to invite them, or happened to stumble upon your church's website. But, if someone they know – someone like YOU – were to personally invite them to join you at an appropriate church event, they probably would come. If you ask them to come with you, to sit with you, if you introduce them to others who are there, if you meet with them after church to debrief the encounter with them, not only will some of them come, but some of them will come back again! Now, they might not sign up after one invitation, but most people will respond if you continue to leverage your relationship with them in a concerted, consistent, personal manner to engage them in spiritual conversations and invite them to church.

This entire process must be covered in a concerted effort of prayer. It's not as if you're doing this on your own, but you're joining in the work that the Holy Spirit is already doing in their hearts and lives – leveraging the spiritual formation opportunities that your church is offering, and working with God, connected with your church, to see a life change brought about in your un-churched friend.

My book, *Mission: Possible – Living the Great Commission* includes an easy to follow six-step missional living plan that teaches you to engage in spiritual conversations with people you already know in an intentional way. It will teach you how to leverage relationships you already have with people around you each and every day to see them become part of Christ's Kingdom.

As a pastor, I am encouraged whenever I see a family bringing a new family to church with them, someone bringing a coworker to church with them, or a new person report that a friend invited them to come to church. I've found that these people are much more apt to stay and become part of the church than those who just happen to "check out our church this week!"

A church can also develop a plan to pray new people into the church. Here a team of people meets together on a regular basis to pray over names of people who need to know Christ, a specific neighborhood in town, or an unreached people group in your area. This prayer is far more effective if it is joined with prayer walks through those areas, tangible acts of service to the people group you're praying about, and people have tools like brochures and invitation cards to hand out to those they're inviting.

If a church wants to employ this effort, then they must demonstrate a concerted effort to pray. This is more than listing this as a prayer request in the bulletin, sending out weekly, or daily, reminders to pray for the lost, or asking the leadership team to be in prayer. There must be an earnest group of people who are willing to meet at least once a week for at least 2 hours to earnestly pray for these people. These prayer meetings must have a listening component to them. Not only are we asking the Lord to work in their hearts, to draw them into our church, but we're asking Him how He can intersect our lives with theirs so that we can engage them in spiritual conversations. This ***WILL*** take us out of our comfort zones. This will cause us to invest in their lives financially, with time, sharing of resources, or other things He leads us to do – ***or all of them***! It will be messy, it will be costly, it will cause us to reorder our priorities, but it will also result in amazing fruit for the Kingdom!

We Need to Look For Fruit

If our goal is to make mature disciples of Jesus Christ who are going to make more mature disciples of Jesus Christ then we have to look for the right spiritual fruit in someone's life. The word "fruit" is often used in the New Testament to represent the "evidence" of our relationship with Christ. Consider the following statements Scripture makes regarding spiritual fruit:

- A true believer shows the fruit of repentance. Matthew 3:8.
- You can tell genuine motives by their fruit. Matthew 7:17-18, Matthew 12:33, and Luke 6:43.
- Those who are not bearing good fruit are destroyed. Matthew 3:10, Matthew 7:19, Luke 3:9, and John 15:2.
- The seed of God brings about good fruit. Matthew 13:23, Mark 4:20, and Luke 8:14.
- You can tell a disciple by the evidence in their lives. John 15:8 & John 15:16.
- Sanctification (being conformed into Christ's image) is evidence of a genuine faith. Romans 6:22.
- We are able to join Christ in His work in the lives of others. Romans 7:4-5.
- The evidence cannot be hidden. Ephesians 5:8-9.

- Our relationship with Christ leads to more righteousness. Philippians 1:6.
- Our relationship with Christ leads us to do good works for Christ. Colossians 1:10.
- God's discipline leads to righteousness. Hebrews 12:11.
- Our relationship with Him leads us to praise Him. Hebrews 13:15.

All of these are good indications, or evidences, that we have a genuine relationship with Christ. The amount of time we spend with Him will increase the yield of His fruit in our lives. While we should not focus on the fruit itself, our focus should be on Jesus, we should desire to be a fruitful disciple of Christ. Our focus on Christ will yield the fruit. If we're happy with a little bit of fruit, we may be no different from the church in Laodicea mentioned in Revelation 3, where Christ says that their ineffectiveness prompted Him to "Spit you out of my mouth!"

Jesus is Going to Ask You About This!

In 2 Corinthians 5:10 Paul tells us that there will be a day when we will be held accountable for how we used all that Christ gave us to build into His Kingdom – or how we used it to build our own kingdom and neglected His. He has given us His Holy Spirit; He has called us, gifted us, led us, and empowered us. There is no excuse for any believer in Christ to stand before Him and say, "I wasn't sure what to do," "I couldn't do it," or "You were asking too much of me." Here in America we have so many resources at our fingertips, we have great freedom to speak His truth, and we have every opportunity to make disciples of Jesus Christ through our daily interaction with others. We must leverage all that Christ has given us to be obedient to His calling on our lives rather than focus on our own lives to the point of neglecting His Kingdom.

I know that there are many who have heard the gospel message and have decided not to give their lives to Christ. I know that Scripture indicates that in the last days many will hear the message and refuse it. I know that people can't know Christ unless the Holy Spirit does a great work in their hearts and calls them unto Himself. I know all of that. But I also know that there is much more that we can do as individual Christians, and together as churches, to make mature disciples who are going to make more mature disciples.

Have we become comfortable in our way of "doing church?" Have we bought into the false teaching that says that good people go to heaven and have we chosen to see ourselves as mostly good people? Have we given the majority of the responsibility to build our spiritual lives to our pastor? Do we expect the church leadership to do most of the evangelizing? Have we fallen into the trap of spiritual complacency – coasting in our relationship with Christ once we saw a little bit of spiritual forward progress?

Be Warned!

The warnings to the seven churches in Revelation 2-3 show us that we are in a dangerous place when we coast in our relationship with Christ. Each of these churches was established on the truth of the Gospel of Jesus Christ, yet only two of them are commended by Christ without criticism. The others are criticized because:

- They have abandoned their first love.
- They have followed the heresy of false teachers.
- They have tolerated the woman Jezebel, who is a seductive false prophet.
- They need to repent of the sin of being ineffective.
- They have become complacent and lukewarm because of the earthly wealth they hoard.

Where are we on this list – as a church and as individuals? Are we one of the two churches that are commended without criticism? They stood firm in the midst of persecution, slander, and tribulation. They walked through the open doors that God placed before them to be salt and light in their cities regardless of the cultural situations surrounding them. Are we worthy of such accolades – or do we deserve to be criticized as the other churches were?

The American Dream

The American Dream promises freedom, equal rights, and opportunity to anyone who wants to take advantage of it. These opportunities have led many to enjoy the kind of wealth that most civilizations afforded only the elite few. In fact, if you have any money in the bank, and have any money in your pocket, you are wealthier than 92% of the rest of the world. The vast majority of the world lives on less than $10 a day. Here in America we can spend that much on coffee in a day! There's nothing wrong with experiencing this kind of wealth, but we have to realize that God will hold us accountable for how we spent it. Are we hoarding it for our own future? Are we foolishly spending it on unnecessary things? Are we wisely investing our wealth and resources into the Kingdom of God?

The American Dream mentality causes most of us to constantly look around at what others possess and covet their possessions. When most families earn more money they spend it by upgrading their home, their car, their clothes, their technology, and their toys. Have we in the church allowed the earthly wealth of the American Dream to cause us to become complacent and lukewarm? Have we bought into the dreams of the world as a compromise to the dreams of the Kingdom of Christ? Are we giving our money away in accordance with biblical directives, or are we hoarding it for ourselves? A quick comparison between the typical American Christian and the typical American non-Christian identifies very few differences in how we spend our time and how we spend our money. If American Christians don't allow the biblical directives regarding our finances to pull us further from the American dream, we will be no different than the church in Laodicea, to whom Christ says, "I will spit you out of my mouth."

False Teachers

False teaching abounds in America today. We have become so Biblically illiterate that we're easily fooled into embracing false doctrines. Many Christian television programs promote the error of their false teachers, who are often very wealthy because of the money those who are watching willingly send to them. They buy luxurious houses, nice cars, take amazing vacations; they even convince their viewers of their need for private jets. This manner of living is far different from that of Jesus, the apostles, and the pattern set by the early church.

How have we allowed false teaching to influence our corporate or personal theology? Bookstores are full of the books written by false teachers who promise wealth and prosperity for those who follow Christ. The relative truth doctrine of our culture has invaded many in American churches today, amending theology and doctrine in subtle – and not so subtle – ways. Age-old applications of Scripture are being challenged by the "enlightened new theologians." Many are being led astray because they spend so little time in personal Bible study, listening prayer, and aren't being discipled by a strong Christian mentor.

The fact that some independent organizations are willing to ordain anyone for $20 through the mail has helped compromise the standard of leadership within many church circles. The high standard of deeper study, accurate exegetical and hermeneutical practices, and a dependence on the Holy Spirit through prayer are being compromised by a "quick and easy" leadership approach. Many church leaders cave to congregants demands to entertain the masses, or increase the bank accounts, more than they stand firm to the calling to make disciples of Jesus Christ.

Keeping Up With The Pace

Do we need to repent of the sin of being ineffective in our own personal relationship with Christ – or as a church? Are we striving for the goals and purposes that Christ gave us in His teachings, in our own personal lives, and through our ministries? Have we replaced those goals with the desire to keep up with the church down the street, or in another city? Are we trying to emulate the programs or preaching we see in larger, seemingly "more successful" churches? Has this desire caused us to be ineffective in fulfilling our goal to make disciples of Jesus Christ?

In the mid 90's the Willow Creek Community Church, located in a Chicago suburb, experienced significant growth under the leadership of Bill Hybels. Many churches sent representatives on a journey to visit Willow Creek and see what they were doing to bring about such growth. Many tried to implement the same programs into their own churches, hoping for similar growth.

In 2007 Bill Hybels published a book called, *Reveal*. In this book, Bill and his leadership team shared the results of an assessment of Willow Creek's process and realized, "We made a mistake." Rather than develop mature disciples of Jesus Christ, their work to grow the church had brought in many "observers" who did not progress in their faith. They did a good job of filling the pews each week, as well as the ministries of the church, but this did not result in the kind of spiritual growth they were expecting. Most of the people were attracted to the crowd level of the church and stayed at that level without developing a life-transforming relationship with Jesus Christ. Many of the churches who patterned their own ministries after Willow Creek's realized that they had invested in the wrong program as well.

I'm all for studying healthy church growth, but what we utilize from the lessons must be done within the boundaries of what we're hearing from the Lord in listening prayer. What works in a Chicago suburb probably won't work in your church. What works in a church of 26,000 people probably isn't going to work in a church of 65-100 people. Studying the principles behind the success other churches are experiencing and then prayerfully applying it in a local context is much different than patterning what we're doing after what another church is doing.

Doing it Right

Two of the churches listed in Revelation 2-3 were doing it right. They were living missionally in their cities. They were advancing the Kingdom in hostile environments. They stood on the truth. They were striving to bring the truth of the Gospel to those who needed to hear it.

Still, Jesus did not have all good news for them. He said that things would be tough for them as they stood on the truth, but He encouraged them to endure. He promised to open doors of opportunity before them that no man could shut! I believe that these same promises are available to us today as we strive to hear His voice and build His Kingdom as we make mature disciples who make more mature disciples of Jesus Christ.

Study Questions
Chapter 6
An Amazing Growth Strategy

1. Would you rather make a convert or a disciple?
2. Have you ever thought about meeting with someone for a year so that you could disciple them? If yes, how did that go?
3. Why do you think that most churches are not experiencing growth?
4. What do you think that churches could do to experience more growth?
5. How many people have you personally brought to church with you this year?
6. How many of them stayed and became productive members of the church?
7. Why did they stay or why didn't they stay?
8. Have you ever been part of a church growth strategy that majored on coming together to pray that God would bring more people in the church? Tell the story.
9. Which of the fruits of discipleship listed on page 135 have you seen in your life?
10. Have you ever considered how modern American Christianity has merged with "The American Dream?" Discuss your observations.

11. Can you name five false teachers that are popular in American culture today? How do you know that they are false teachers?

12. What steps do you take in your life to ensure that you're doing discipleship the right way?

CHAPTER 7

ONE-ON-ONE DISCIPLESHIP PLAN

"You then, my child,
be strengthened by the grace that is in Christ Jesus,
and what you have heard from me
in the presence of many witnesses
entrust to faithful men who will be able to teach others also."
2 Timothy 2:1.

As we've discussed throughout this book, I believe the purpose of any Christian ministry, including the general purpose of the church, is to complete the Great Commandment (Matthew 22:35-40) and the Great Commission (Matthew 28:16-20). To love God, love others, share the Gospel, and make disciples who make disciples.

The purpose or process within any organization doesn't just come about on its own. It is intentionally developed over time through prayer, study, discussion, implementation, and assessment. If we look at the intentional process that Jesus used to teach, love, challenge, and train His disciples we see that everything He did and said had purpose. One of His primary purposes was to develop them into disciples of Jesus Christ who demonstrated maturity in spiritual disciplines, and were effective in Kingdom service.

Jesus spent more time with His disciples than He spent with anyone else. This wasn't just because they were the ones who were traveling with Him. He had an intentional plan to train them for the ministry responsibilities He knew He was going to give them when He returned to His Father in Heaven. The Gospel accounts clearly show the intentional pattern Jesus followed: spend some time with the crowd, more with His followers, even more with His disciples, and the most with the inner "core group" of disciples. John's Gospel gives us a great glimpse into the one-on-one time that he spent with Christ and the lessons He learned through that personal interaction.

Much of what we experience in churches today is closer to the temple model of the Old Testament than the early church model demonstrated by the apostles. I believe that one-on-one discipleship is the ultimate goal that Jesus Christ had in His personal ministry with His disciples, but it is one of the most absent aspects of ministry in the current Christian church model. Most churches are based on the one-to-many model that group preaching and teaching exemplifies. Lasting spiritual formation best takes place on more intimate stages - and there is no more intimate stage of discipleship than a one-on-one relationship. Jesus demonstrated this in His own life and ministry, and the apostles began the early church with a solid discipleship model in place. I'm not sure where this model became derailed, but I've found this to be a new concept to many who have been in the church for decades. Today, many people are not willing to open their lives to this stage of intimacy and transparency, but we must if we are to develop trust and solid teamwork among one another.

These one-on-one spiritual discipleship relationships give us the best chance to dive into the deep spiritual waters that a close, personal, intimate relationship with Jesus Christ can offer us. The personal attention of a mentor, the opportunities for personal introspection, and the customization of a personal learning plan open the door for radical spiritual growth – growth that is only limited by the amount of work the student is willing to put into the study. These one-on-one relationships open a pathway that can lead to a deeper commitment to Christ, to the local church, to evangelism, to missions, and to all of the components found in a mature Christian walk. These relationships are also the best way to learn the disciplines of faith, develop leadership skills, answer tough questions, develop close friendships, and they help any believer take steps towards a more mature faith.

Real-Life Stories

As I've worked to refine this process in my own life and ministry over the past twenty-some years I've been amazed to see the rapid, radical spiritual formation that can occur when a teacher spends one-on-one time with a student.

I began to notice this very thing in my own discipleship experience. I grew up in the church. I attended church on Sunday mornings between 50-52 weeks a year. We would take one week off of church to go on vacation (and it would seem so strange not to be in church on Sunday) and I would have the occasional sick day, but for the most part I was always in church on Sunday morning. I didn't complain about it. I liked it. It was a place where I was around friends and adults that cared about me.

My family usually got to church on time (or early), we stayed for Sunday school and church, and we were there for all the special gatherings throughout the year. We came back for most Sunday night services, as well as mid-week gatherings. I was part of the kids club, came to VBS, graduated to youth group, went to every retreat offered, attended summer camp, and anything else that came my way. I read my Bible and prayed, and read books about God from time to time. All of this added to my faith week by week, but none of these are the things that I can point to as "quantifiable spiritual formation" in my life. I don't remember the outline of a single sermon, a single lesson plan, a single "special guest speaker's message." They all added to my faith week by week, but none of them stand out as a "life changer."

What I do remember are the dozens of conversations I had with two spiritual mentors who took the time to answer my questions, recommended books to read, talked with me about what I was learning, prayed with me, and showed me what it was to become a man of God. I credit them for helping me through a tough period as a young man and for keeping me on the path the Lord had for me when there were plenty of others who were attempting to pull me in other directions. Sure, I made mistakes (usually when I disregarded their advice or direction), but the Holy Spirit didn't allow me to stray far. These mentors were there to pick me up when I sinned, help me get right with the Lord, and make forward progress in my own discipleship journey once again.

As an adult, there were two pastors who were instrumental in helping me respond to God's calling to enter ministry full-time. Both of them spent dozens of hours discipling me. We met together to talk, to pray, to walk through life together, to work within ministries together, and to wrestle with the tougher questions about life as a disciple of Jesus Christ. I don't remember any of their sermons, either. I don't remember any of their Sunday school lessons. I remember the hours we spent talking, digging deeper, and praying together. I remember when each of them said, "You know, I think Jesus is calling you into full-time ministry."

You might say, "Seriously!?!? You don't remember a single sermon or Sunday school lesson?" There are a couple that stand out over the past 48 years of my church attendance, but those aren't the times that I point to as the transitional experiences of my life. Even if I could point to the sermons that moved my heart, it was the debriefing that I had with my spiritual mentors that really cemented what I was hearing through the sermon or lesson that I remember. The one-on-one time meant much more to me than the large group time.

So, you might ask me, "What role do I see the Sunday morning sermons, the Sunday school lessons, the small group discussions, and the variety of ministries we labored at side by side playing in my discipleship process?" They played many crucial roles. The sermons and lessons were part of my spiritual formation. One sermon after another taught me truths from Scripture week by week – as well as how to apply them to my life in general terms. The Sunday school classes taught me even more. Although I can't quantify the specific lessons I learned in those contexts, I know they provided the soil in which the one-on-one discipleship time was planted, grew, and blossomed. They were the material that many of our conversations covered. They got my mind going on a topic or a question and the one -on-one time allowed me to dig deeper into it, look at it from a number of angles until my mind could grasp it, allow me to dissect it and file it in my brain in a way that I could reference it and teach it to others at some point in the future.

I honestly don't think that I'd be a pastor today if it wasn't for the time these four mentors spent with me one-on-one. I would be like so many others who sat and listened to hundreds of sermons without knowing how to respond. I would be afraid to raise my hand to ask the questions. I would struggle to apply biblical truths to my life and fail until I gave up. My questions would remain unanswered. My challenges would be left on the table. My spiritual gifts remain untapped. The Lord's calling on my life would have been left in the category of "could have been" with so many other ideas that jumble around my brain.

I'm not sure if these four people set out to intentionally disciple me. I'm not sure if I just turned out to be the one with all the questions, the one who bugged them until they spent more time with me, or the one who was willing to do the homework assigned, hand it in, and actually get it graded. As a teacher, it's easy to spend time with the student who comes to your office, who stays after class to talk about what was covered, and who does the extra reading assignments. I was that kind of a student and I got bonus time with almost all of my teachers as a result.

As I entered full-time ministry I wanted to be that same kind of a mentor to those I was ministering to. I wanted to intentionally answer their questions, help them work through life's problems in a way that brought honor and glory to Jesus Christ, teach them to read and study the Bible, pray, and delve into other spiritual disciplines. As I offered these things I was surprised to see how many of them took me up on the offer. Many of them showed a hunger and thirst for the deeper things that our group gatherings couldn't satisfy. I quickly realized that I didn't have enough time to be available to meet with them at their pleasure. I had to develop a structured plan to be able to meet with them and disciple them if I wanted to do this well.

As I've implemented this plan and seen its success I've shared it with others and they too have been able to see its success in their lives. So, now I'm sharing it with you.

One of the men I met with for about a year to disciple one-on-one told me that he learned more in one year of meeting with me than he did in 30+ years of church attendance. We met once a week for about an hour. That was less than the time he spent in Sunday morning worship and Sunday school each Sunday. It was less than the time our small group met each week. It was less than the time we spent attending and serving with another ministry each week. Add all of those up, and he was with me at church almost seven hours a week. Yet he didn't credit ***that time*** as contributing to his spiritual formation the most – no, ***the one hour*** we spent once a week for a year was what made the biggest difference in his life.

That compliment shouldn't be given to me because of my amazing knowledge, my outstanding wisdom, or the incredibly deep academic insight I brought into each of our sessions! NO! That compliment goes to the success of the process of the guided learning that he was experiencing as we were responding to the leading and working of the Holy Spirit in his life. I was just guiding him, helping him hear the voice of the Lord, and helping him figure out how to apply what he was hearing from the Lord to his life. I answered his questions, offered him challenges, and helped him step-by-step along the way.

Another guy I met with for about a year had a similar story. He had grown up in the church and been around Christians his whole life. He had sat through hundreds of sermons and Sunday school lessons. He read some of the books and watched some of the videos his pastors and teachers recommended. As he transitioned from teacher to teacher he began to receive a number of mixed messages. He had a lot in his brain and his heart. The problem for him was that all of the learning was disconnected and he couldn't find the way to connect it all in his own mind. This disconnect caused him to struggle to figure out how to make it all apply to his life. He had all of this head knowledge that only benefitted him when someone asked a question in an area he had studied during a Sunday school class or at another church function. When someone would say, "So, what do we do with that?" He would just shake his head and say, "I'm not sure" and defer to someone else who could help with application.

The Holy Spirit used our time together to help him figure out what do to with all the knowledge he had accumulated. As we sifted through the competing theories and challenged the false doctrines together he was finally learning how to read and study the Bible to determine where the truth stood. Then, we talked about how he could apply that truth to his life. It wasn't a far step for him then to learn how to lead others to hear the leading of the Holy Spirit as he desired to help them determine and apply biblical truths in their lives as well.

I don't really think that a sermon or a Sunday school lesson could have done that in this guy's life. I don't really think that another book on this theory or that theory would have helped. He needed someone to sit down with him and work one-on-one to help him figure out the truth and prayerfully learn to apply it to his life.

The most common comment I receive from those I am meeting with is, "I've learned more about _____________ in the time I've met with you than I have in X number of years at church." My response, "Of course you will. You've spent hours in concerted prayer, study, and discussion on _____________ topic." Each person would fill in the blank on their own. It could have been prayer, sanctification, the work of the Holy Spirit, how to read the Bible, how to lead someone to know Christ, how to answer questions other people have about God, how to reconcile what the Bible says with what some scientist said, or a variety of other topics. Many times people came to me with a list of difficult Bible passages that they needed help working through. We tapped into a good study Bible and worked through them together. I was doing more than just answering their questions. I was teaching them how to dig deeper and answer the questions on their own. I was introducing them to good resources and letting them find the answers to their questions as the Holy Spirit was speaking in their life.

I could tell you dozens more stories, but I'll just move along to identify what I started to do in my one-on-one discipleship sessions and allow you to prayerfully determine if this paradigm will work in your situation as well.

Key Aspects of One-On-One Discipleship Relationships

I've learned a number of things about the dynamics of a one-on-one discipleship culture as I've read on this topic and I've put it into practice in my own life and ministry. While these observations might not apply to every situation, I've found they apply to almost every situation that I've come across personally. I suggest that you will find that they will apply to most of the situations that you will encounter as well.

The Holy Spirit is the Teacher

While one person usually takes the lead in a one-on-one discipleship relationship, we have to remember that the Holy Spirit is the teacher. He will teach both people through the discipleship process. The person taking the lead should never hold the perspective that they have "reached the apex of discipleship progress" and is now teaching those who have climbed the mountain to learn from the master teacher. No! Mutual humility before each other and humility before the Lord is a key aspect in a one-on-one discipleship relationship and will lead both people to hear the leading and teaching of the Holy Spirit.

The Goal is to Become Like Jesus

Both people need to have the goal of using the discipleship relationship to strive to become more like Jesus Christ. While there may be certain spiritual disciplines, or attributes, that a spiritual mentor might exemplify, or try to teach to the person being discipled, both people need to remember that these are just disciplines or attributes that are pointing us towards Christ and conforming us more into His image. Any discipleship process that takes the focus off of Christ, His Holy Written Word, spiritual disciplines found in Scripture, or the application of biblical principles, has moved away from being about Jesus and will no longer see true spiritual fruit.

The Basics

Those wishing to grow through a one-on-one discipleship relationship are meeting together on a regular basis for the purpose of growing in their relationship with Jesus Christ by learning from one another. Meeting times consist of reading, studying, working through issues, discussion of application, prayer, service projects, etc. The learning environment here is one-on-one so it can be completely customized for each student and the learning becomes intense because it is completely focused on that one student. We are answering their questions. We are discussing the topics they're interested in learning. They don't have to wait their turn. They're not going to check out because what we're covering is review for them. They're invested. They're focused. They're learning and growing right where they are in their own personal journey.

There are two different dynamics for these one-one-one discipleship relationships. The first is as a mentor and a student. There is a clear distinction between the one who is leading and the one who is learning. Here the mentor has selected a student to spend one-on-one time with or the student has sought out the mentor to teach them one-on-one or to challenge them to go deeper into an area or discipline. The mentor will be the one who is selecting the material to be used and guiding the process. Both will learn as the Holy Spirit works through the reading, the discussion, and the times of prayer, but there is a clear difference between the one who is the mentor and the one who is the student.

The relationship looks a lot like an academic advanced degree program. Resources are selected and used to help the student grow in one or more areas of their spiritual disciplines. Homework is given and growth is assessed on a one-on-one level. The time spent with the student allows for radical, personal, specialized spiritual growth to take place at a level contingent on the student's own personal investment. If the student is only willing to spend 15 minutes a day reading through the resources being used their learning will be limited. If the student is willing to spend two or three hours a day their learning will really accelerate. They get to choose their level of learning based on their own level of investment. The teacher's involvement doesn't change. The teacher works with the questions the student has discovered, the truths they've uncovered, and we continually steer the learning in the direction the Lord is leading.

I usually recommend that the student try to spend about 30 minutes each day working through the materials we're using. The homework being assigned may look overwhelming if the student is trying to work through it all at once, but it's not very difficult to work through if they spend time on it each day. I think this is a truth about anything in life. Tasks look overwhelming if we try to accomplish them all at once, or too quickly. By asking the student to whittle away at the resources a little bit each and every day I'm giving them a paradigm of learning that is very doable. I often challenge them to look at something they can give up in order to fit these 30 minutes into their day. It's often a TV show, some time on Facebook, or they divert some time reading other things in order to make time for the material I've chosen to lead them down this learning path. If they're having a hard time finding 30 minutes in their day I ask them to take a time inventory for a week. I have them write down what they're doing in 15 or 30 minute intervals each and every day that week. Then we look at their inventory together and it's usually easy to see what things they can give up in order to invest some time on their studying. I've yet to find someone who really wants to learn who can't possibly find time to fit 30 minutes into their day. There have been some who have told me they weren't going to give up a TV show or some of their time online and therefore couldn't fit my assignments into their schedule. This was a good indication that they weren't ready for this kind of a learning environment. I asked them to pray about it and meet with me again in a few months to see they were able to find the time then.

The second option is for two people who are at the same level of spiritual formation who come together for mutual learning. This may be two members of a leadership team who are doing a study to prepare to share it with others. It may be two friends who wish to do a deeper study on a topic being covered on Sunday morning, in a Sunday school class, small group, etc. It may be a couple who are seeking to delve deeper into an area of their marriage, parenting, or who just wish to explore the depths of a relationship with Jesus together.

Whatever the reason for discipleship, whatever the dynamics of the two people who are meeting together, these guidelines will aid you as you seek to grow in your relationship with Jesus Christ together.

Church Attendance is Important

I am, and always will be, a big fan of the church. Not all churches. There are plenty that are not standing on the Truth of Christ's Written Word. I would have you avoid those churches. I'm talking about the organization that Christ established as the gathering of His people to worship Him, to do His work, in His timing, and using His ways. I will never advocate for a ministry, a program, or a plan that is designed to ***go around*** His established church.

Maintaining a healthy long-term discipleship relationship with the church is crucial – for both the mentor and the student. The one-on-one time should never be seen as a replacement for the church, but an enhancement to it. All areas of church interaction are beneficial in the development of discipleship and will eventually benefit from the growth as disciples mature and want to give back to the ministries of the church.

I long for the day when more churches embrace this one-on-one discipleship culture – building into it and leveraging its fruit. This can be mutually beneficial for the church as a whole, the ministries within the church, and the people who call the church their spiritual home. Large gatherings have their place. Classes to teach The Written Word of God are crucial. We need small groups. But we also need mature disciples of Jesus Christ discipling others to be mature disciples of Jesus Christ. Mature disciples typically look for ways to invest in the Kingdom through serving others through the local church, which is something that most churches are desperately seeking.

Stick With Same Genders

It is so important that men disciple other men and women disciple other women! I've been flexible on this point a couple of times in the past and found that it was a mistake each time. I'm not flexible on this point anymore. The only exception I now have happens when there aren't enough mature female disciple-makers to begin working with the women of the church who are seeking someone to disciple them. In this case, I, and/or an elder, work to develop a few disciple-making female leaders and ask them to reach back and disciple others after 3-6 months of training. During this time I have heightened security measures in place to ensure that we don't fall into the pitfalls outlined below.

Of course, this point would also not apply to couples who are seeking to do deeper study into areas that will benefit their marriage or family.

The relationship that develops between two people who are in a one-on-one discipleship relationship is quite powerful. This process will contain times of Scripture study that will lead both people to share intimately from their hearts. They will talk about their pasts, share some hurts, and hopes for the future. They will pray together, cry together, worship together, and in the process they grow closer to Jesus Christ and to each other. They may have experienced healing, seen spiritual breakthroughs, seen miracles take place, or other amazing things. These things change people and they change relationships. We want to make sure that these relationships don't cross any inappropriate boundaries.

God has designed us to be connected to others in three ways: spiritually, emotionally, and physically. Whenever we are in a relationship that is developing spiritual or emotional intimacy there is a strong pull to have physical intimacy as well. When two people have connected in any two of these areas the third is bound to follow. Scripture is quite clear that physical intimacy is reserved for a husband and a wife in a godly marriage. Developing an expectation that men disciple men and women disciple women will help protect against the development of inappropriate areas of emotional or physical intimacy.

Because our culture is embracing same-sex sexual relationships more and more, discretion and accountability need to be shown in any discipleship relationships to ensure that we don't cross any biblical or ethical boundary lines. The oversight of your pastor and/or elders can play a crucial role in the protection of the people involved in any one-on-one discipleship relationship.

You Have to Intentionally Spend Time Together

This may sound like an obvious point, but I think it needs to be said. Time together is crucial in the development of any relationship between two people and a discipleship relationship is no different. I ask to meet those I'm discipling once a week or once every other week. If they choose to meet once every other week I'm sure to make contact with them during the week we're not meeting as well. We might meet through a brief Facebook or email conversation, a phone call, a video chat, or personal time spent together. We also spend time together at church. Church attendance, Sunday school, and small groups become the perfect place to worship and grow together in addition to the one-on-one time you're spending together.

The face to face meeting time should happen at least once every two weeks and should last for an hour or more. You must be intentional about the time you spend together. If you start chatting about your family, work, sports, the weather, TV, movies, etc. you'll find that most of your "discipleship time" has been spent talking about other things. If this is the case, your time to pray, dig deeper into God's Word, or wrestling with practical application is going to be cut short. Remember, you're not getting together to talk about sports or to share the latest gossip. You're not getting together to be pals. You're not getting together to talk about your hobbies. You're getting together to talk about Jesus. Give Him the honor and respect He is due and schedule other times for you to get together to cultivate your friendship apart from your discipleship conversations.

I recommend that you plan to meet together for 60-90 minutes. If you meet for less than that, you probably won't have enough time for your conversation to get to the depth required, or you'll cut out something important such a prayer or the discussion of practical application points. I know we live in a rush, rush, rush society, but discipleship isn't something that can be rushed. It requires you to unplug, disconnect, take a deep breath, slow down, and quiet your heart before the Lord in prayer, in Scripture reading, and in conversation with each other. Turn off the phone, hit your Wi-Fi button, turn off the TV, and spend focused time before the Lord together.

Some have suggested that we get together for half a day just once a month. I can see why this might be an easier thing to schedule, but I recommend every week or two to maintain continuity between meetings. If you only meet once a month you may have a hard time remembering what you talked about the last time you met (I know that I do!), and you might spend a good deal of your meeting time getting caught up to where you were. Perhaps you're better at maintaining continuity over time than I, or perhaps your schedule only allows you to meet together once a month. You could give any schedule a try and assess how well it works for you. The important thing here isn't that you ascribe to my recommended pattern, but that you are regularly growing in your relationship with Christ in measurable ways.

The Length of the Relationship Has To Be Agreed Upon

The modern church model has a long-range discipleship plan: come to church for the next 30 years and we'll teach you what it means to be a follower of Christ. This model just can't meet the personal needs of every single person right where they're at today. What happens if someone wants to identify and develop their spiritual gifts, but that class is only offered every 2 or 3 years? What happens if the 100-level students drag their feet and create a dynamic where Sunday school teachers or small group leaders never really get past the basics of faith? It's those who are seeking the deeper things who usually get left out.

I've found that discipleship relationships work best when they last six months to one year. This typically gives enough time to adequately assess where the student is in their faith, find out what their next steps are, develop a customized plan for learning, and implement that plan. The learning plan must take into account their stage of discipleship, their capacity for learning, and their own personal interests. Then, as stages of development progress, there is more time to go one level deeper or identify a completely new area of study. Often this new area of study will require us to agree to renew another six month commitment to meet together.

I've found that setting up a short-range limit for our time to meet together forces both of us to be more intentional in the time we spend together. We all are procrastinators at heart. We run the risk of putting the important things off if we think that our relationship together is going to go on for a long time. Just as college has a set date on which a semester ends so teachers and students know when they have to get their work completed, setting an end date in my discipleship relationships helps both of us set a proper pace for our time together. Sometimes we accomplish our learning plan earlier than I expected and we stop meeting together before the six months we initially planned to meet. Other times I have underestimated the amount of work that our time together is going to require and we have to extend the time beyond our original plan. It's okay to be flexible, but if you just set out without some kind of expectation or plan for an end date you're going to find that the relationship tends to drag on with limited results. Remember the lesson learned through having to think through the six-day scenario? You can't drag your feet or waste time if you're only meeting for 6 months! You have to be very intentional with the time you have together.

Our Time is Limited

Each one of us only has so much time available to meet with people each week. We all have work and family obligations that we have to attend to each week. We have to leverage our available time in a way that allows us to accomplish the most fruit for the Kingdom.

I begin all one-on-one discipleship relationships with two or three "exploratory sessions" in which I clearly outline my expectations for our time together and determine if the person I'm meeting with is going to honor those expectations. I give them a few homework assignments and see how well they complete them. I ask them to get their hands on some resources and see if they acquire them before our next meeting. If they're going to honor my expectations and the work I've assigned, then GREAT! We'll get a lot of work done in the next six months. If they're not going to honor them then I'll determine if I'll continue to meet with them, hoping that they'll increase their commitment, or knowing that they're going to ***learn something*** as we meet together – even if it's less than they would be learning if they were fully committed to the plan. My schedule dictates if I'm going to continue with meet with those who are hesitant to make a full commitment. If there are others who are willing to meet with me with a full commitment, then I believe that my time would be better spent encouraging the less committed to seek someone else to meet with and engage with those who are willing to fully invest their time and effort in meeting with me. I know that doesn't sound like a nice thing to say, but the very fact of the matter is that I only have so much time I can spend meeting with people one-on-one. I want to leverage that time to reap the most spiritual fruit, so I have to set expectations and be prayerfully discerning regarding those I meet with.

What Areas of Spiritual Disciplines Do You Study?

Many people don't even know where to begin if you ask them what spiritual disciplines they want to work on first. You might have to ask them some probing questions. Do they want to see their prayer life go to a deeper level? How about learning to read and study their Bible? How about understanding prophecy? Do we do a Bible study together? Do I spend time answering the questions they have as they do their own study? Do they need to learn how to share their faith with those around them?

There are so many areas that we ***COULD*** study. How do we know where to start?

I ask some establishing questions to determine where they are in their walk with Christ and what discipleship areas they're willing to put the time and study into. I ask about their own personal devotional life, their prayer life, their involvement in the church, and how they interact with Christians and non-Christians outside of the church. If I'm meeting with someone I already have a relationship with I will probably already have a good understanding of most of these things, but I always like to hear their take on them as well. I'm prayerfully seeking the answers to the following questions for my own assessment of our one-on-one time together: Where are they in their faith? What do they want to learn? What are their next steps? What things have to happen to bring them to the next stage of their spiritual formation? The answer to these questions is dependent on the particular person. There is no one discipleship program that can possibly meet the needs of every individual person being discipled. We have to be flexible. We have to be creative.

Here ae some of the establishing questions I often use:

- Tell me how often you read the Bible.
- Tell me how much time you spend when you sit down to read the Bible.
- Tell me how much life transformation comes from this time you spend with the Bible.
- How much time do you spend in prayer?
- How much time do you spend engaging in listening prayer?
- What does your attendance at church look like? How often are you here? What ministries are you part of? What are you learning during these times?
- I will use the two assessment tools that I mentioned in Chapter 1, the amended *Growing a Healthy Church* chart and

the Engel Evangelism Scale, to let them do their own assessment. Then I strive to verify and affirm their answers.

- Have they identified any spiritual gifts in their life? How are they using them?
- I will ask them to identify someone around them who exemplifies what spiritual maturity looks like and ask them why they identified that person.
- I encourage women to read Proverbs 31 and identify how their lives compare.
- I ask men to read 1 Timothy and identify how their lives compare.
- I ask them to "paint a picture" of what they want their spiritual lives to look like in five years.

If, after an initial discussion and period of prayer, I'm still not sure what direction to head, then I begin with a basic study. I start with a book like *Crazy Love* by Francis Chan or *The Pursuit of God* by A.W. Tozer – or a book of the Bible such as Colossians, Ephesians, or John. As they are going through this initial study I can usually fine tune an area of learning during the discussion we have as they report on their learning.

What Tools Do We Use?

One of the great aspects of this model of discipling is that there are thousands of resources I can use to disciple those I am meeting with. Most of the tools I use are books that I have read, videos that I have viewed, and sermon series that I have preached or appreciated myself. I also use books of the Bible that pertain to a person's area of interest. The tools you use need to be customized for each of the people you are discipling. The ministries in your church, or a neighboring church, could be a great tool to use as well. Sometimes we go to a conference together, do a prayer walk together, or meet with another person. The key is to be flexible and prayerfully follow the leading of the Holy Spirit.

Books are by far my favorite resource to use when I disciple others. Here are a few reasons I like to use books as my primary discipleship tool. I've found that books are:

- **Easy to find** – I find that Amazon.com and Amazon Kindle are great resources.
- **Inexpensive** - Many of the books I recommend are available for less than $5.
- **Non-consumable** – We can use them multiple times and I can use the same material to disciple multiple people without having to personally review similar material multiple times.
- **Handy** – The student can read them at their own convenience.
- **Patient** – The student can go over the same material again and again and again until they "get it" without taking any more effort on my part.
- **Lasting** – The wisdom in books can be passed down from generation to generation.

In essence, a book is like having the author available to you on your own schedule. He or she is available to teach you, over and over again if necessary, truths that have been prayed over, thought about, tested, tried, and proven to be true. The book can always be within an arm-reach, be paused when needed, be re-started anytime, and can be passed to someone else who needs to hear its message.

A word of warning!!! There are a number of popular authors in our culture today who are writing half-truths and false theology. I never use a resource that I haven't tested myself. If someone brings a resource to me that I haven't heard of I always go through it myself before using it as a discipleship tool. If I use a tool that is teaching false things then I have to double my effort to reverse the false teaching and replace it with the truth. Two outstanding resources I use to check potential books are equip.org and carm.org. Equip.org is part of the ministry of Hank Hannegraff – the Bible Answer Man. A major part of his ministry's focus is to identify false teachers and false trends in fake American Christianity. Many people get caught up in catch phrases and flashy presentations. I call this "bumper sticker Christianity." Equip.org digs deeper, goes behind the scenes, and does an outstanding job of comparing what they're finding as they investigate authors or televangelists with what they find when they investigate Scripture.

The other website I often use is carm.org. It's the website of the Christian Apologetics and Research Ministry. They too act as a watchdog organization, investigating the claims of organizations who claim to be Christian and comparing what their spokespersons say to what Scripture has to say.

Quite often I'm given resources that sound good on the surface but turn out to have twisted theology at their core. I want to stay far away from these resources! There are dozens of articles on each of these websites that are easy to search and reference to help you steer clear from these dangerous resources as well.

We live in a world where everyone has an opinion, shares their opinion, and expects everyone else to agree with their opinion. It doesn't matter how informed that opinion happens to be, how much research has been done to support it, nor do we suggest the correct view or interpretation that should be used to develop an informed, rational approach. From time to time one of the resources on my "approved list" takes criticism from someone I'm discipling. After doing my own research into the claims against the resource, I always use this time to build into their discipleship by teaching them how to test a resource, a teaching, or a teacher. I'll point them in the direction of equip.org or carm.org and ask them to investigate what they heard for themselves. As they report on their research at our next discipleship meeting we both learn from their experience. Most of the time their research affirms the validity of the resource we're using, but from time to time I decide to remove a resource from my recommended reading list because of the information they bring to me.

One time a person in the church brought criticism against a book I was referencing in a sermon series. They pointed me towards a blog post condemning the resource we were using. After doing my own research to test the validity of these criticisms, I printed out the criticism and brought copies of it to my small group. I asked them to get into groups of three and research the validity of the criticisms with me. They found that the critical article misquoted the book, took Scripture points out of context, and did a really bad job of putting intention into the author's work that really had no place there. Not only did the group come out of the experience with a deeper trust for the book we were using, but they were learning how to make an honest assessment of others' criticism in a healthy way.

My Book List

My book list is nothing more than a list of books I use to disciple others. These are the resources that work well with my process. If you ask others who are engaged in discipleship relationships to share their book list with you I'm sure you'll find many additional resources on their list. In fact, I often ask others who have their own discipleship process to share their resource list with me so that I can expand the list of books I'm using in my own discipleship relationships.

Prayer is the most important aspect in the selection of a resource to use to disciple others. Let the Holy Spirit be your guide as you seek His direction in this process. My list might be a good place for you to start, but there are dozens of other great books and videos for you to use.

There is a difference between using a ***book of the Bible*** and a ***book about the Bible*** in the discipleship process. I choose to primarily use a book of the Bible to help people learn doctrinal truths and books about the Bible to help people learn how to apply those truths. Of course, there is some overlap here, but I'm shooting to use a good blend of Scripture and application as I disciple others.

Here are some books that I've found are a good place to start:

The Pursuit of God – A.W. Tozer

The Fourfold Gospel – A.B. Simpson

Crazy Love – Francis Chan

Experiencing God – Henry Blackaby

The Purpose Driven Life – Rick Warren

I've had great success in handing books like these to people I'm discipling and asking them to use the interactive logging technique to take notes. (I outline this note-taking technique in a paragraph below.) Then, as we meet together to debrief what is being learned, I have a very good idea what direction to take as we move forward. We must pay close attention to what they're learning, how they're learning it, and asking the Holy Spirit for discernment regarding the next steps. Then, as they make more progress, we can guide them to the next resource or person who can disciple them further.

Sometimes the student will get through the entire book, other times we begin with a resource and then redirect to another. Don't stick with a resource that isn't working. Don't be afraid to change resources in an attempt to find something that better connects with the student you're discipling.

See Appendix A for a complete list of recommended resources I regularly use as I disciple others.

Commitment to Homework is a MUST!

One-on-one discipleship is not an attempt to replace the spiritual formation that happens at a 100, 200, or 300-levels. We are not preaching to a crowd, we are not teaching multiple people in a classroom, we are not gathering together with a small group to learn from one another – we are meeting one-on-one to intentionally guide the learning experience for one student. Just as in the case of a college setting, to do this the mentor must assign homework and spend a good deal of time assessing the student's response to that homework.

As I meet with those I'm discipling, the majority of our time together is spent going over the notes they've taken while they were doing their homework. I'm not summarizing what the author said in the chapter they were reading. I'm not doing the work for them. I'm not giving them shortcuts. I'm guiding them through their own learning journey.

I use the "interactive logging" technique that is outlined below. I've found it to be an excellent tool to give me a good understanding of the learning process the student is using. It helps identify questions they have as they go through the resource they are studying, and it allows them to "teach me" what they've learned as they engage in their own study. Every student is going to get something different from a resource. This technique allows the Holy Spirit to do the teaching and it helps me as I strive to guide them through the process of hearing His voice.

Interactive Logging

Interactive Logging is a technique for taking notes that I learned while going through the Alliance Ministerial Study Program (MSP) – it's a home study seminary designed for those entering full-time ministry with the Christian and Missionary Alliance as a second career. The MSP is a mentor-driven learning experience. I worked through dozens of assigned resources on my own and met with my mentor to share the questions that I had and the lessons I had learned as I was studying on my own.

In this technique the reader goes through the assigned books on their own while taking thorough notes. If they come across a passage they're struggling to understand they may write something like, "I just don't get the fourth paragraph on page 5. What does the author mean here?" If they come across a new concept that wrecks their idea of God and builds their faith big time they might write, "Page 12, paragraph 2. Wow! I've never seen this before. This makes so much sense to me."

When the student and mentor meet together most of their time together is spent processing through the student's interactive log. The mentor takes time to answer the student's questions, listens to their "Aha! Moments" to ensure they got it right, and then they work together to learn to apply what the student is learning to their everyday life.

The student doesn't have to remember what they were learning from memory – can any of us really do that well? I don't have to cover material that they knew already or that they got with little effort. Here the learning directly pertains to their level of understanding and their need for application.

Sometimes I ask the person I'm discipling to email their log to me before we meet so that I can see the progress they're making and know what direction to take the conversation, or we can just go over the logged points together as we're meeting each time.

The great thing about using books to disciple is that I don't have to be the one doing all of the teaching. They are spending one-on-one time with the author, and they're able to learn at their own pace. They can pick up the book once a day for 30 minutes at a time, or dive deeper for a 3 or 4 hour session. The time they choose to spend with the author of the resource they're using doesn't infringe on my own personal schedule at all. This way I can disciple several people concurrently with this same technique. We meet once a week – or once every two weeks – and they're the ones doing the majority of the work.

I've posted a brief overview of the interactive logging process for you to use with those you are discipling on the Acts of Light website. Just go to www.ActsofLight.com and pick on the books link on the left hand side. You'll find it with the other materials listed for this book. You can download it and print it out for your own personal discipleship use.

When I am incorporating interactive logging in my discipleship process I always give the person I'm working with a short passage of Scripture to interactive log as a first homework assignment so that I know they're properly using the technique before we begin to study a book together.

Ministries of a Church Become a Tool in the One-On-One Discipleship Process

Corporate worship is an important component of the discipleship process. It should be a personal spiritual discipline of both mentor and student. Sunday school attendance, small groups, and other ministries of the church are also important components. As mentors we can use ministries of the church as part of our discipleship process by choosing to meet others at church ministries and events as a tool to help them learn rather than as the entirety of their learning process. Perhaps we will need to attend Celebrate Recovery with someone for a year, or go through a step study with them, sit in a Sunday school class with them so we can dig deeper into those topics during our one-on-one time together during the week. Perhaps we have to sit with them during worship to teach them specifics of the experience, watch their kids in the nursery so they can truly connect without distraction, or take good notes on the sermon so that we can debrief with them as we meet during the week. Maybe we need to invite them to attend our small group so they have a great chance to interact with others in a close, personal learning environment. Maybe they need Christian friends and we can invite them to an appropriate event or ministry of the church that will help them make some healthy friendships.

This is a great perspective to take with someone who is not a good reader or doesn't have the time to sit through a video series. They can use the same Interactive Logging technique to take good notes during the service, Sunday school class, small group, or other ministry time, and you can go over those notes when you meet with them during the week.

What Does our Time Together Look Like?
There are typically seven things I strive to accomplish each time I meet with someone I'm discipling:

1. Greeting.
2. Opening prayer.
3. Determination of the amount of work they've done.
4. Review of their interactive log.
5. Discussion on points of theology or application.
6. New homework assignment.
7. Closing prayer.

Greeting

After a short time of greeting one another (just a couple of minutes) I move into our first time of prayer. These times together can turn into a "friendly chatting session" all too easily. This isn't time to talk about the weather, what's on TV, or how well the Sabres are doing. This is time to dig deeper into God's Written Word and we want to give Jesus the respect of using this time well – as well as being respectful of both of our own personal schedules.

Opening Prayer

I always begin our meeting time with prayer. I pray for our time together, for the learning process, for wisdom and discernment, and blessing over the person I'm meeting with. I look at this as a way to set the pace for the discussion to follow.

Assessment of Their Work

I ask for a review of what they have studied since the last time we met. This is an important question. If they report they have been reading, studying, and logging we dig into their notes. If they report they haven't had the time to read, study, or log, then I encourage them to make time to read, study, and log and ask them if they have any questions from their log that we didn't cover last time.

If they don't have any questions from their log, then I gently tell them that we're just going to close out our time with some prayer. I kindly refuse to take up our time that was supposed to be set aside for discussion on deeper study points, on application, and prayer and use it for anything else. I've learned that it is very important for the mentor to set the parameters for the learning environment and stick with them throughout the time we meet together.

A few years ago I was in a one-on-one discipleship relationship with Dan Scarrow. He was serving as the Director of Leadership Development in the Central District of the Alliance. I learned quite a bit from him in the times that we met together. The primary purpose of his position was to help me become the best pastor I could possibly be. He set up a meeting with me, gave me homework, and asked me to bring it with me to the meeting. After our discussion on the homework he assigned I asked him what he would have done if I didn't complete my homework assignment. He replied, "I would have closed our meeting with prayer, set up another date to meet, and encouraged you to complete your homework."

At first I was taken aback by his curt answer and the curt manner in which he presented his answer. After a moment processing the concise way he presented his reply I added, "And if I didn't do my homework the second time?"

"Then I would have told you that you're not ready for this kind of learning. I would have set up a date six months from now for us to meet again and asked you to pray about if this is the right kind of a thing for you to be involved with. If you weren't prepared that time then you be bumped to the end of the list of guys interested in meeting with me."

We only have so much time in our day. Our lives go by so quickly. There are so many things that demand our time and attention. We are investing our time best if we meet with those who are willing to dig in deeper and do the kind of work we're expecting them to do. I know it's not a popular thing to say, but if you're not willing to invest in a one-on-one discipleship relationship then I'm going to choose to spend my time with someone who is.

Review of Their Interactive Log

Next, I ask them to go through their interactive log notes with me. I've found that if they've done their homework they ***always have questions***. We work through them together. They almost always have issues with what they've read. We work through them together. They usually have a few "Aha! Moments" to share. We rejoice in them together. They usually need some help applying what they're reading to their personal lives. We work through those points of application together.

Reviewing the persons interactive log helps to cement their own personal learning process and affirm that they can read and study on their own. They've read on their own, they've written down important points, and now by having to explain what they've read and learned to me they are proving to themselves that they've learned these points. Many times people say, "Wow! I didn't realize I learned that." Or "Wow! I guess I really do get this now!"

This portion takes up most of our meeting time together, but the time goes so, so quickly! I have to keep my eye on the clock so that I hit the brakes on our conversation in time for us to pray together. Depending on our schedules, I may extend the conversation on their interactive log. Most times we have to put the discussion on hold, pick it up next time we meet, or pick it up on Facebook later on in the week.

Discussion on Points of Theology or Application

One of my chief concerns as I disciple others is that the spiritual formation that is taking place is firmly grounded on proper theology and appropriate personal application. As we discuss their interactive log points I take notes on areas of theology or personal application that I wish to delve further into later in our meeting time – or right as we're discussing their interactive log. Quite often this is to contradict the meaning of a point they got out of the book, when I would have a different perspective than that of the author, or when we need to dig deeper into proper personal application points.

I look at this time as a chance to leverage what they've learned to teach them deeper things. Quite often the author has got them thinking in a direction, but hasn't provided the opportunity to explore that train of thought any further. Sometimes the application the author presents isn't the best way to apply the biblical truth to our personal lives. I'm trying to be sensitive to what the Holy Spirit is saying to the person I'm discipling and join with Him in the work of spiritual formation. I've found that many of my students look forward to this time of clarification, teaching, and affirmation. It strengthens our discipleship relationship and gives me a chance to feel more "hands on" in the process. I'm not just "listening to what they've learned," but I'm able to build off of what they've learned and help them take the next steps in their journey.

Homework Assignment

The typical homework assignment is "Keep on reading and logging." But there are times when our discussion has brought up a point that we need to explore a little more and I'll take them on a little detour. This detour usually involves reading Scripture to clarify points of theology or application.

One time someone was having a hard time letting go of some habitual sin. I asked them to read and log the book of Colossians every day until we met again. They really needed to hear Paul's admonition at the end of Colossians 2:

"Since you died with Christ to the basic principles of this world, why, as though you still belonged to it, do you submit to its rules: "Do not handle! Do not taste! Do not touch!"? These are all destined to perish with use, because they are based on human commands and teachings. Such regulations indeed have an appearance of wisdom, with their self-imposed worship, their false humility and their harsh treatment of the body but they lack any value in restraining sensual indulgence." Colossians 2:20-23.

The assignment of reading this same book of the Bible over and over again really helped to take some steps to unlock the grip sin was having in their life. The mentor has to be in tune to the leading of the Holy Spirit as they are seeking the right homework assignment to use.

Closing Prayer

I always end our one-on-one discipleship times with prayer – this time with both of us praying. I believe that praying with someone is one of the greatest ways to assess their relationship with the Lord. Here, I'm listening for them to make a connection between what they've learned and application into their own lives. This is a time for confession, for the start of repentance, for thanking the Lord for the things He's teaching us, and for beginning (or continuing) His work in our hearts.

I usually ask the other person to begin this time of prayer so that I can use my time of prayer to affirm the things that they are learning from the Lord and ask Him to continue to bless this learning process for both of us as we continue on this discipleship journey together.

Leveraging Spiritual Gifts

This model also leads to the possibility of identifying "experts in areas of discipleship" within the church. This might be an area the Holy Spirit may have gifted them, an area they have personally studied, or an area of skill they have developed over the years. One-on-one discipleship can leverage their gifts to benefit those who are seeking to learn more about these same gifts. I can recommend the person I'm meeting with begin to meet with someone else who is more adept in a spiritual discipline, which both frees me up to meet with someone else and gives other people in the church the blessing of discipling in the areas of their spiritual expertise.

For instance, if one person in our church has a powerful prayer life then they can be instrumental in discipling others to learn how to have a powerful prayer life as well. They can work one-on-one with dozens of people over time to teach them to model the prayer life they have developed. We don't want to create a model where everyone has to be great at everything. We also don't want to create a model where people hold onto their skill because they're afraid of others mastering a spiritual discipline as well as they have

We must strive to meet the New Testament model of being a body, a team, or a family. We must rely on each other. We must build into our strengths, use our spiritual gifts, trust the Holy Spirit will continue to gift us, and work together to build everyone up. In fact, quite often, our own spiritual skills grow as we teach others. Our own spiritual muscles are stretched, challenged, and changed as we are forced to grow ourselves as we teach others.

There is a difference between the Holy Spirit gifting someone and someone who learns a skill on their own. As with all areas of discipleship, our goal is not to replicate what the Holy Spirit is doing, but to allow the Holy Spirit to do His work in us and through us. The key here is listening to the leading of the Spirit in prayer, Bible study, and our discussions together.

Potential Pitfalls of Meeting One-on-One

I've already addressed the inappropriate emotional or physical intimacy pitfall that comes from studying with someone of the opposite gender. Here are a few other potential pitfalls that have to be considered:

1. **Just being a friendship**. It's so easy for these one-on-one sessions to be nothing more than time together as friends. Our entire time could be spent talking about family, weather, sports, politics, TV, movies, music, etc. If these meetings are to be used to develop spiritual formation then the focus must be intentionally kept on spiritual formation.

   It's the mentor's responsibility to ensure that this time is being used for spiritual formation. You might want to set up a few times to get together for just friendship during the duration of your one-on-one discipleship, but you have to guard the content of your meeting times.

2. **Turning into counseling sessions**. You are not a professional counselor. These are not professional counseling sessions. Your discussions will get into issues, hurts, sins, false teaching, and mistakes from someone's past. Some of our discipleship discussions will offer counsel to help someone move forward in their walk with Christ, but we have to guard

against defining our discipleship by continually talking about someone's problems, issues, or struggles. We may offer a listening ear, some helpful biblical advice, and prayer, but we must respond differently if there are issues that keep coming up. Then it's probably time for you to recommend that they see a professional counselor regarding that specific issue and move on to other discipleship topics in your own discussion times together.

It is crucial for you to follow the Holy Spirit's leading in this area. If, while you are praying, you are sensing that you're over your head in this area, then you it would be a good idea for you to get some advice from your own mentor before making any recommendations to the person you're discipling.

3. **Getting over your head theologically**. Your discipleship discussions will probably get into the deep waters of theology. It's easy for you to get in over your head. During these times your default mode might be to fake it so that you don't look bad to the person you're discipling. Don't fall into this trap! Learn to say, "I'm not sure about that. It's a bit over my head. Let me get back to you on that." Write down some good notes of your own, check with a mentor, and then follow up. The last thing you want is to go down a bad path theologically and become a proponent of false teaching.

   The best part of writing down a question that is over your head and seeking out the advice of a mentor of your own is that you now know the answer to that question, or clarification in that area of theology, for the next person who asks it. You're learning, they're learning, and both of you can pass that learning onto the next person you disciple.

Elder's Oversight

The best way for you to ensure that you're not going down an unhealthy path in your one-on-one discipleship is to seek the oversight of an elder or a pastor. They will be a good resource to you theologically, they can probably offer good recommendations for the right resources to use, and they will provide good accountability to ensure your relationship operates in a healthy paradigm.

Study Questions
Chapter 7
One-on-One Discipleship Plan

1. Is there someone in your life who met with you one-on-one to disciple you in the past? Tell the story and the impact that relationship had on your faith.

2. Have you ever met one-on-one to disciple someone who was further behind you before? Tell the story and the impact that relationship had on you and the person you were meeting with.

3. Much of this chapter outlines a process by which you can meet with someone. Did you find the chapter to outline a doable process for you? Why or why not?

4. What benefits do you see in using books of the Bible or books about God as a major part of a one-on-one discipleship process?

5. What other tools do you think would be helpful to use?

6. Are you familiar with a note taking technique that is similar to the interactive logging technique? How does it work?

7. Do you see how ministries of the church can be used as a discipleship tool?

8. Have you ever used a ministry of the church as a discipleship tool in the past?

9. Can you add to the potential pitfalls listed at the end of the

chapter? What can be done to ensure we don't fall into them?

CHAPTER 8

REACHING FORWARDS AND REACHING BACKWARDS

"Be imitators of me, as I am of Christ."
1 Corinthians 11:1.

The spiritual formation process the Holy Spirit is leading us through can be compared to going on a spiritual journey. There are many people who are ahead of us on the path which begins when we are new in Christ and heads towards becoming a mature, fully-devoted disciple. We can learn from those who are ahead of us on this journey. They have many spiritual lessons to teach us, plenty of amazing God stories to relate as they trusted Him, and they have developed many spiritual disciplines over the years. There are people who are right next to us on the journey. They're discovering similar spiritual truths, learning to apply similar spiritual disciplines, and trying to overcome similar spiritual barriers. There are also many people who are behind us on the journey. They're experiencing things very similar to those we experienced, asking questions similar to those we asked, and are experiencing struggles very similar to those we've overcome. They are looking forward to days when they're further ahead in their own spiritual journey.

While each of us walk on this journey on our own pace, this is not a solitary journey. We experience many others on the path. We can learn from those who have gone ahead of us, encourage those who are walking with us, and teach those who are behind us. The journey is much easier for each of us if we depend on those ahead of us, help those who are around us, and reach back to teach those who are behind us. We must be intentional if we want to accomplish Paul's challenge to the church in Corinth:

"Do you not know that in a race all the runners run, but only one receives the prize? So run that you may obtain it. Every athlete exercises self-control in all things. They do it to receive a perishable wreath, but we an imperishable. So I do not run aimlessly; I do not box as one beating the air. But I discipline my body and keep it under control, lest after preaching to others I myself should be disqualified." 1 Corinthians 9:24-27.

We should strive to run the race of discipleship well. We should strive to get as far in our own spiritual formation process as possible in our lifetime. We should always be working on developing more spiritual formation, never thinking that we've achieved enough or that we have more time in the future to put more time and effort into the journey. As we mature in our faith we should make a goal of developing the leadership qualities required to serve the Church of Jesus Christ as a ministry leader, an elder, a board member, or respond to a call to full-time Christian service. To do this, we must position ourselves to learn from those who are ahead of us, find encouragement from those who are running the race alongside of us, and we must reach back to help others in their own journey as well.

Understanding the Process of Spiritual Formation

In a book entitled, *Invitation to a Journey: A Road Map for Spiritual Formation*, Robert Mulholland argues that every disciple of Jesus Christ has to progress through four phases of spiritual formation in order to make it to the next stop on our spiritual journey. While our end goal is to become fully-devoted, mature disciples of Jesus Christ, there are many milestones that we have to pass to make our way to that destination. Here is an illustration of those four phases:

The first phase is called "**Awakening**." During this phase we have an "Aha! Moment" when we discover that there is more to experiencing God than we've previously experienced or understood. This personal revelation might be a deeper understanding of a specific attribute of God, an area of sin in our lives that needs to be dealt with, a new spiritual discipline for us to develop, a level of stewardship to experience, or an area of leadership for us to step into. This new discovery may be met with wonder and awe, fear and trembling, or both. It takes some time for us to sort through this new awakening and what practical application it will bring in our discipleship. Once we wrestle with acknowledging that it's time for us to take the next steps in our spiritual journey required to respond to this new awakening we progress to phase two…

Phase two is "**Purging**." During this phase the Holy Spirit shows us one part of our life that needs to be amended in order for us to take the next step in our spiritual formation. He might point out sin that we've been holding onto, false teaching that we're not willing to allow the truth of God's Holy Written Word to erase, our reluctance to take the step required to develop the spiritual disciplines He's calling us to, or that we're too busy to commit to step up into a leadership role. This isn't an easy phase for any of us to go through. Our sinful nature struggles to hold onto the things that are not of God. We battle against old habits and beliefs – some of which may have been with us for a long time. Some of us may have been carrying these things for most of our lives. This is the most intense part of the spiritual formation process as the Holy Spirit attempts to convict us of our sin, convince us to trust Him, and lead us to the next phase. As we learn to trust Him completely this phase becomes easier for us. When we finally throw up our hands and say, "Ok! I'm letting go of my life – YOU take control!" we're able to progress onto the third phase…

Phase three is "**Illumination**." We have finally allowed the Holy Spirit to get us past the barrier of purging and now we're seeing that He was indeed right. We're experiencing the freedom from the sin we gave to Him, we're drawing nearer to Him as we're practicing new spiritual disciplines through the Holy Spirit's leading, or we've stepped up into a leadership position and we're seeing the fruit of our investment in the Kingdom of Christ. At this point most of us say things like, "Why didn't I do this years ago?" or "I was so foolish to fight the Holy Spirit!" or "Why did I hold onto that sin so tightly?" As we gain more and more confidence walking with this fresh new relationship with Christ it leads us to the fourth phase…

Phase four is "**Union**." We know we're in this phase when we've walked far enough with this new relationship with Christ that we have made it become a permanent part of our spiritual lives. These spiritual disciplines have become part of our regular spiritual routine and we're seeing the fruit of them on a regular basis. We've gained victory over the sinful areas of our lives to the point where they're not as much of a temptation to us anymore. We've stumbled through the new experiences He's led us into well enough that we're willing to engage with them without much reservation. We've stepped up into a leadership role that is a really good fit for us and we're seeing the fruit of our service in the Kingdom. We're able to move forward in our spiritual life with a firm confidence that this change is for keeps and we're confident we'll never go back to where we used to be.

BUT WAIT! There is a barrier between phase three and phase four that is that is called, "**The Dark Night of the Soul**." Yes, it is as foreboding as its moniker implies. It's a difficult time, it's a struggle, it's a battle to truly embrace the lessons we've learned (or are learning) and we MUST push through this barrier before we're able to make any more spiritual progress. The Dark Night of the Soul causes us to question the validity or importance of the spiritual awakening we've experienced. Satan will attempt to convince us that we're better off going back to the place where we're comfortable, that this kind of change in our lives is too hard, or unnecessary, and that we're much better off leaving the spiritual formation to the pastors and missionaries and just live our comfortable lives and simply focus on our church attendance.

WARNING! The easy thing to do when we experience this time of testing is to take a step back, to seek a place of comfort, and to allow the lies of Satan to convince us that we're okay in this safe place. After all, God shouldn't lead us to difficult things, right? We look around us and we see plenty of others who haven't responded to the things we thought God was calling us to do, so we question the validity of the calling. We might think that the spiritual formation calling is just for the "professional Christians" around us. You know, the pastors, missionaries, and ministry leaders in the church. Maybe we feel that we've bitten off more than we can chew. We might allow the thought that we're overzealous to slip into our minds. Maybe we seek the opinions of those who hold a lesser faith than we have and find that they think we're crazy to try these new things. Maybe we determine that it wasn't the Lord that was calling us to this next level in our lives. Satan will turn up the volume on any one of these thoughts and attempt to convince us that we're better off staying where we are. The longer we park ourselves in one place the bigger the victory he has in our lives.

As you develop into a more mature disciple of Jesus Christ you will come to realize that this time of intense testing is a natural and necessary part of spiritual formation. Then you can look for it and acknowledge it as a sign that you're making spiritual forward progress. In fact, this is ***a positive sign*** that you're heading in a good direction! This probably won't make going through a Dark Night of the Soul any easier, but it will allow you to see God's hand in it – and hopefully you'll reach out and take His hand to help you through it. It helps to keep in mind that God has good things for you on the other side of this barrier.

Once we've pushed through the Dark Night of the Soul and are truly experiencing union with God, He once again leads us to another deeper truth about Him and we experience our next Awakening. This leads to another time of Purging, a time of Illumination, another Dark Night of the Soul, and a deeper Union with Him. This process continues over and over again – each time leading us to a more intimate relationship with Him.

Everyone is Somewhere

Every one of us is at one specific place in this spiritual formation cycle at this very moment. Perhaps you can easily identify where you are even as you've been reading this section. Sometimes we need to depend on the wisdom of a spiritual mentor to help us determine where we are and how we get to the next phase. In fact, each of us is ***always somewhere*** in this spiritual formation process. We might be confidently making our way into the next phase, battling to surrender something to the Holy Spirit so we can move on, basking in the new union with the Lord, seeking His hand to lead us through the Dark Night of the Soul, or we might have been stuck in one place for quite some time. Hopefully, you're making continual forward progress in a timely manner – even if it's slow progress – progressing through each of these phases on your journey.

Spinning our Wheels

One of the toughest things for me to do as a pastor is help someone realize that they've been stuck in one phase for quite some time. It's difficult for me to see their regret as I help them realize that they've been spinning their wheels for years, or stagnant in their faith for years, or have been disobedient for years. I've helped some see that they've been fighting the Lord and refusing to take their next step for decades. I've talked with a few who have been refusing to make forward progress for most of their lives. Some of them are willing to pull up their sleeves and do the work the Holy Spirit is leading them to do in order to begin moving forward. Sadly, many of them are not willing to trust Him to help them move forward and they decide to stay where they are – in that comfortable place of Christian mediocrity.

I'm convinced that many have experienced an awakening with the Lord, progressed through a stage of purging, and made it to illumination, but have then made it to their first Dark Night of the Soul, totally freaked out, have taken a step backwards to a safe place, and have remained there for most of their spiritual lives. Maybe they were told that everything in their lives was going to be better, or easier, now that they've "prayed to receive Christ," and what they're experiencing isn't matching what they were told. Maybe they read their Bible every once in a while, pray over their meals, and go to church every week. They see others with a deeper relationship with

Christ, have tried to develop these disciplines on their own, experienced the Dark Night of the Soul, and stepped back. Perhaps their embarrassment or frustration has kept them from seeking help pushing through. Maybe they don't see any spiritual mentors around them who can help them. Maybe they've surrounded themselves with others who have taken that step back and have agreed, along with the others, that they're going to remain where it's comfortable.

Everyone needs help on this journey of spiritual formation! This is why I believe it's so important for us to develop a disciple-making culture, where reaching forward and reaching backwards are a regular part of being a disciple of Jesus Christ!

As a pastor, I hope to see those I lead go through at least one iteration of these phases each and every year. I challenge everyone to submit to a spiritual formation process, intentionally including a 100, 200, and 300-level learning environment, as well as being part of one-on-one discipleship relationship to help identify the leading of the Holy Spirit and encourage one another through the process of spiritual formation in their lives. We were never made to go on this journey on our own. Each step of the journey is much easier when the leading of the Holy Spirit is met with guidance from someone ahead who is helping to map the way and others around us encouraging us to follow His leading every step of the way.

Developing a Disciple-Making Culture

Mature disciples of Jesus Christ who have been discipled to an advance level of biblical learning and application should be reaching backwards to intentionally disciple others, who will grow in knowledge, maturity, and become effective in service, and then will reach backwards and intentionally disciple others, and so on. I call this, "developing a disciple-making culture." In this culture, spiritual growth will take place exponentially and the intentional focus of reaching forward to learn and reaching back to bring others forward will create a natural flow of spiritual formation that will continue with very little maintenance from leaders. It is crucial for the spiritual leaders in any church or ministry to be the ones who are leading the spiritual formation culture that the 300 and 400-levels exemplify. If they are not, and this disciple-making culture takes root, then they will quickly be outpaced by those who are submitting to what the Holy Spirit is doing in the lives of those who have submitted to this disciple-making culture. A focus on true discipleship will lead to evangelism, and evangelism will lead to a need for further true discipleship.

I believe that if a church or ministry can establish a disciple-making culture, seeing at least 10-15 men and women intentionally discipling others who are behind them in the journey, the culture of the church will be revolutionized and it will begin to experience exponential growth. Those being discipled will reach back to disciple others, and those being discipled will reach back to disciple others, and so on, and so on, and so on.

In a disciple-making culture evangelism and discipleship are not just "programs" that need to be developed and maintained. These crucial areas of healthy church ministry are now part of the underlying culture found within the lives of those who are part of the church or ministry. In this culture it's much more than one or two leaders who are striving to make disciples – many people within the church or ministry are intentionally reaching forwards to learn, alongside to encourage, and then backwards to teach. Dozens of people are meeting together one-on-one each week to pray together, share together, learn together, develop deeper spiritual disciplines together, and to reach out to advance the Kingdom through evangelism as they demonstrate Christ's love to others in tangible ways.

I get excited every time I talk about the great potential to change a city that a disciple-making culture provides the people within any church or ministry. Church leadership who embrace and develop this kind of a culture are growing their congregations, planting new churches, and sending their people to live their lives missionally each and every day. A disciple-making culture will bring about healthy growth. First, spiritually, within those who are being discipled, then numerically, as those who are being discipled reach out to those who don't yet know Christ.

Study Questions
Chapter 8
Reaching Forwards and Reaching Backwards

1. Have you ever been taught the phases of spiritual formation?

2. Can you relate a story of a time that the Lord brought you to a new awakening in your spiritual life?

3. Can you relate a story of a time that the Lord brought you through a time of purging in your spiritual life?

4. Can you relate a story of a time that the Lord brought you through a time of illumination in your spiritual life?

5. Can you relate a story of a time that you experienced a dark night of the soul?

6. Can you relate a story of a time that the Lord brought you through a time of union in your spiritual life?

7. Look at the four phases. Where do you think you are at this point of your spiritual journey?

8. What do you think your next steps are?

CHAPTER 9

HOW DO I GET STARTED?

**"Brothers, I do not consider that I have made it my own.
But one thing I do: forgetting what lies behind
and straining forward to what lies ahead,
I press on toward the goal for the prize of the upward call of
God in Christ Jesus.
Let those of us who are mature think this way,
and if in anything you think otherwise,
God will reveal that also to you.
Only let us hold true to what we have attained.
Brothers, join in imitating me,
and keep your eyes on those who walk according
to the example you have in us."
Philippians 3:13-17.**

I hope this book has helped you define what it means to be a fully-devoted, mature disciple of Jesus Christ and how you can be actively involved in making more disciples of Jesus Christ who make even more disciples of Jesus Christ. I hope you found the one-on-one discipleship plan to be one that would be easy for you to implement in your own personal life and ministry. I hope you intend to find someone ahead of you on their spiritual journey to meet with you so that you can learn from them, that you will encourage those who you find are alongside of you on your journey, and that you will intentionally and prayerfully find someone who is behind you to meet with to disciple one-on-one.

You might be wondering, "How in the world do I get started?" There are so many people, there are so many resources, and there are so many options. Or you might be thinking, "How am I going to find the time to do something like this?"

I challenge you to pray, seeking the Lord's leading in your response to this material. I hope you will at least pray about someone who is ahead of you on the journey who you can meet with to learn from. This will likely lead you to encourage others around you and learn to reach back to others who are behind you. As you strive to dig deeper into the Word on your journey to be a mature, fully-devoted disciple of Jesus Christ He will lead you on your next steps of reaching back to help others. You might have to step outside of your comfort zone to contact a spiritual mentor, initiating a time to meet with them, but things will get easier after that first phone call, email, text, message, or chat after church on Sunday morning. Share what you've learned from this book. You could recommend that your mentor read this book. Talk about what you hope to gain out of a one-on-one discipleship relationship, or what you have to offer. Develop a plan and begin to implement it – one step at a time.

Finding Someone Ahead of You

It is crucial for you to find someone ahead of you for you to continue growing in your own faith as you disciple others. Here are some suggestions of those who are already around you who may be delighted to meet with you on a one-on-one basis:

- Pastors.
- Elders.
- Sunday School teachers.
- Ministry leaders.
- Prayer warriors in your church.
- Someone who knows their Bible really well.
- Someone who demonstrates the kinds of spiritual disciplines the Lord is calling you to develop.
- The first person you think of when someone asks you a question like, "What person in this church knows Jesus Christ the best?"

As a pastor, I welcome the opportunity to meet with people one-on-one to disciple them. I have structured my schedule to allow time each day to meet with two or three people for the purpose of one-on-one discipleship. I am thrilled when someone knocks on my door and asks it would be possible for me to meet with them one-on-one to help them grow in their faith. I'm sure your pastor would welcome the opportunity as well. Even if they're too busy to meet with you, they'll probably have good recommendations for someone you can meet with.

I know many elders and ministry leaders who would love to meet with people in their church or ministry one-on-one. This is one way that current elders or ministry leaders identify potential future elders and future ministry leaders. The time spent one-on-one becomes a great training and interview for future leadership roles within the church or ministry.

Someone Alongside of You

It's relatively easy to find someone alongside of you to meet with for prayer, encouragement, and mutual study. This search process needs to begin with prayer, asking the Holy Spirit to clearly identify someone. You can ask Him to put someone on your heart, or bring someone into your day that needs encouragement, or both. Then look around you on church on Sunday morning, your Sunday school class, or small group for three or four weeks, looking for those who are demonstrating steady attendance, who are asking questions that are very similar to yours, and who appear to be in similar stages of life – or in their spiritual journey. This might also be a good question for your pastor, elder, or ministry leader. In addition to joyfully helping to disciple you, they will be glad to hear that you're looking for someone at your own stage of your journey to meet with for prayer, study, and encouragement.

Someone Behind You

Finding the right person behind you might be the most difficult of the three to find. While it might be easy to identify those who are behind you in their faith, you're really looking for someone who is behind you, but who isn't satisfied staying there. Someone who is going to be excited about meeting together, consistent in their commitment, and who is going to do the homework required for deeper study. Just as I outlined above, this process needs to begin with prayer and remain covered in prayer as you proceed.

Many of those behind you might start out with good intentions, but quit after just a few sessions together. This is why I start out with a two or three "exploratory sessions" in which I continue to outline my expectations and determine if the person I'm meeting with is going to honor those expectations. If they're going to honor them, then GREAT! We'll get a lot of work done in the next six months. If they're not going to honor them then I'll determine if I'll continue to meet with them, hoping that they'll increase their commitment, or knowing that they're going to ***learn something*** as we meet together – even if it's less than they would be learning if they were more committed to the process. My schedule dictates if I'm going to continue with meet with those who are hesitant to make a full commitment. If there are others who are willing to meet with me with a full commitment, then I believe that my time would be better spent encouraging the less committed to seek someone else to meet with and engage with those who are willing to fully invest their time and effort with me.

I have learned that the best way to identify those who are ready to meet with me is to outline what one-on-one discipleship looks like in a sermon series, in a Sunday school class, during counseling, or as I get to know new people in the church, then I offer to meet with anyone who is interested and I see who responds to the offer. Those who are willing to make the commitment are easy to identify after our first few meetings together.

I realize that most of you who are reading this book are probably not pastors, elders, or ministry leaders, so you're not going to have the opportunity to preach a sermon series, teach a class, or bring this up in your counseling sessions! Just as in looking for someone who is beside you, finding potential people to meet with begins with prayer, discussions with your pastor or elders, and moves on from there.

Asking Good Questions

I've found that someone who is asking good questions – in Sunday school classes, in small groups, on their Facebook posts, or in random conversations – will probably be a good candidate for one-on-one discipleship relationships. Much of the one-on-one process involves asking and answering questions. I've found that asking questions is one of the primary indications that someone is growing in their faith. Seeking out someone who is asking good questions will probably be a great candidate to begin with.

Connecting With Good Students

Someone who has proven to be a good student of God's Word is a good candidate for a one-on-one discipleship relationship because of the amount of personal study and homework that is involved in this model of a one-on-one discipleship process.

Ask yourself questions such as:

- Who's at church each week?
- Who's always there for Sunday school?
- Who's always engaging in the discussion during small groups?
- Who's always part of the ministry that you attend?
- Who do you see with their Bible open, digging deeper at each of these places?
- Who do you notice post good biblical quotes and discussion starters on Facebook?

These are great indicators for you to look for as you pray for someone to meet with.

Pray About It

I cannot over stress how important it is to cover this entire process in prayer!!! We should begin the process in prayer, prayerfully implement the process, and pray for His work to be done in us and through us throughout the entire process.

- Prayer about who we should meet with.
- Prayer about which resources to use.
- Prayer asking the Holy Spirit to do the work that only He can do in our lives.
- Prayer over areas of our lives that are exposed through the process.

- Prayer seeking indications of when our one-on-one time should end.
- Prayer regarding who we should meet with next.
- Prayer for evangelism.
- Prayer for spiritual growth.
- Prayer in every other area of this process.

There are so many areas of discipleship to pray for! In fact, we must cover every area of discipleship in prayer – both ***for*** the person you're meeting with and ***with*** the person you're meeting with!!!

Chapter 5 covered the topic of learning how to hear the voice of God speaking in your life. Learning to hear His voice is a crucial first step to follow His leading throughout the process. If hearing the voice of the Lord is a new thing for you, then I recommend you seek out a spiritual mentor who can help you develop this crucial spiritual discipline in your life as a high priority in your own spiritual formation process.

Leaving a Disciple-Making Legacy

In Matthew 13, Jesus tells the Parable of the Sower and the Seeds. In this parable He promises an amazing return on our spiritual investment when we intentionally sow seeds of the Kingdom into the lives of those around us. Jesus promises a return that is 30 fold, 60 fold, or even 100 fold. Do you realize…

- 30 fold is a 3,000% return.
- 60 fold is a 6,000% return.
- And 100 fold is actually a 10,000% return!!!

I used to wonder how it was even possible to have this kind of a return on our spiritual seed sowing efforts. Most teachers have learned through experience that the lessons they're teaching their students probably won't take root in their lives for quite some time. Every once in a while we're able to see them get to the "Aha!

Moment" that we covered in the last chapter, but those moments are few and far between for most students. In fact, in the intentional spiritual formation plan I implement as a pastor, I only expect to see a student experience a significant "Aha! Moment" once a year. I may not even notice the spiritual formation that is taking place week by week, lesson by lesson, conversation by conversation – these things might have to pile up before the Holy Spirit uses them to bring about the "Aha! Moment" we're all looking for.

A farmer knows that there is a time to prepare the soil, a time to plant the seeds, a time to care for the seeds that have been planted, and a time to reap the harvest. A farmer can't cause the seeds to grow – only God can do that! When we submit to these same principles in the spiritual formation process we gain the amazing blessing of seeing a spiritual harvest for our labor.

I used to wonder how it was possible to see a return of 3,000%, 6,000%, or 10,000% on my spiritual investment, but after devoting myself to discipling others for more than 30 years I am seeing what Jesus was talking about. I am seeing those I discipled discipling others who are discipling others who are discipling others. I am seeing those I led to Christ stepping up into full-time ministry roles, lay ministry roles, and discipling their children in their homes. I am hearing how my sermons, lessons, and writings have taught others Kingdom principles, have challenged others to live these Kingdom principles, are hearing stories of the fruit of their obedience to follow the Holy Spirit's leading. They tell me stories of sharing the lessons they've learned through me with others, of passing my books and blog posts onto others, and the fruit those others have experienced because of it. From time to time I sit back and try to get a glimpse of the extent of my discipleship influence and I'm amazed to see how much God has used me to build His Kingdom. Who am I that He is even mindful of me, let alone that He would use me as a tool in His hand to build His Kingdom? This is one of the things that pushes me to interact with more people, push through difficult times in leadership, and spend the hundreds of hours it takes to write and publish writings such as this one. I'm investing in the Kingdom. I'm tilling the soil. I'm planting His seeds into the lives of others. I'm caring for the seeds that have been planted. And I'm working with the Spirit to harvest the spiritual fruit.

And so can you.

Everyone can invest in the Kingdom of God. There are people ahead of you that you can learn from. There are people alongside of you that you can encourage. There are people behind you that will greatly benefit from the time you spend helping them make their way past the journey milestones that you've gone by.

You Are Standing on Go!

Each one of us has to start from where we are. No matter where you are there are people ahead of you, people alongside of you, and people behind you. You might be a pastor, an elder, board member, or ministry leader. There's still someone ahead of you. You might find them through your denomination leadership, through a local ministerium, or you might have to learn through digging deeper into the writings of deep thinkers and theologians of the past and present.

You might be someone who has been going to church all of your life, but can't really remember a time you were engaging in a one-on-one discipleship relationship. This might be new for you, but you can do it. There was a first time for everything you've ever done in your life. You can do this for the first time too!

You might be someone who is new in your faith. As you look around you might see dozens of people who are ahead of you. Reach out to one of them. You might have to look a bit harder, but you'll see others who are new in their faith around you as well. For you, those you reach behind to help will probably be those who don't know Christ yet. You can be a valuable tool in the hands of the Lord as you share your own personal story with them, encouraging them to give their lives to Him as well.

Ready, Set, Go!

Well, this is the end of this book. Now it's time for you to pray about who you can meet with one-on-one: one ahead of you, one alongside of you, and one behind you.

Ready. Set. Go and make disciples of Jesus Christ!

Study Questions
Chapter 9
How Do I Get Started?

1. List the spiritual mentors that the Lord has put in your life.
2. Which of those mentors do you see meeting with others one-on -one?
3. List five people who are walking side-by-side with you in your spiritual journey.
4. Which of them have you met with personally to learn from each other?
5. Name someone who posts good spiritual discussion questions or comments on social media.
6. Name someone who asks great questions in a Bible study, Sunday school class, or small group you are part of.
7. Do you desire to leave a disciple-making legacy? How well do you think you have invested in that legacy to date?
8. What are your next steps to better invest in that legacy?
9. What's keeping you from taking those steps?
10. Spend some time praying about someone in your life who can disciple you and someone you can disciple. Who does He bring to your mind?

11. What is keeping you from meeting with each of them one-on-one to learn yourself and to teach someone behind you on the journey?

APPENDIX A

RESOURCE LIST

The following is a list of resources I've used to expand my own personal walk with Christ and effectiveness in ministry. I've also used them to disciple others in their walk and effectiveness as well. Any resource has its benefits and limitations. The key is to leverage the benefits and look past the limitations. Just about any resource can be used to develop deeper discipleship. Just about any resource can get in the way of developing deeper discipleship. Pray for the Holy Spirit's wisdom as you use these resources, as well as others that you know of, and others that have been produced since the time of this writing.

The starter books are helpful to get a bearing on another direction to head as you determine deeper areas to pursue, other spiritual disciplines to develop, or specific leadership attributes to be developed.

I am always adding to this list! I recommend that you develop your own list of resources as you're discipling others. Be sure there are others in your life who are teaching you by feeding you resources for your own personal study. If these resources are beneficial for you, they will probably be beneficial for others too, and you can add them to your list.

Prayer is the most important aspect in the selection of a resource to use to disciple others. Let the Holy Spirit be your guide as you seek His direction in this process. Don't be afraid to switch up before you're done reading a book or using a resource. You're better off admitting that the resource isn't working as well as you hoped than to try to finish it with little return.

Starter Books

The Purpose Driven Life - Warren
Crazy Love – Chan
The Pursuit of God – Tozer (Free on Kindle)
Not A Fan - Idleman
Radical – Platt
Got Questions? Jesus Has the Answers! - PJ Bogoniewski

Deeper Walk With Christ

Experiencing God - Blackaby
Celebration of Discipline – Foster
Basic Guide to Eschatology: Making Sense of the Millennium – By Erickson
Perspectives on the World Christian Movement – Winter
The Fourfold Gospel – Simpson
Walking in the Spirit - Simpson
The Gospel of Healing – Simpson
Don't Waste Your Life – Piper
Erasing Hell - Chan
Revival in the Rubble - Kitchen
Fresh Encounter – Blackaby

Kingdom Journeys – Barnes
Sun Stand Still – Furtick
Mere Christianity – Lewis
The Cure – Lynch
What's So Amazing About Grace – Yancey
Mission: Possible – Completing the Great Commission – PJ Bogoniewski

Prayer

Power Praying - Chotka
The Prayer of Jesus – Hannegraff
The Art of Listening Prayer – Barnes

Holy Spirit Dependence

Wholly Sanctified –Simpson
Untamed Christian – Unleashed Church – Wardle
Forgotten God – Chan
Baptism With the Holy Spirit – Torrey
Fresh Wind, Fresh Fire - Cymbala

Deeper Bible Study

How to Read the Bible for All Its Worth – Fee and Stuart
NIV Harmony of the Gospels – Gundry
Look for a good New Testament and Old Testament Survey text.

Healthy Church Ministry

Spiritual Leadership – Blackaby
Sticky Teams – Osborne
The Missional Church Quest – Becoming a Church of the Long Run – Ford and Brisco
Growing a Healthy Church – Spader

The Prayer Saturated Church - Sacks
Purpose Driven Ministry - Warren
Historical Drift - Cook
Spiritual Leadership – Sanders
Tribal Leadership – Logan and King
Making Ideas Happen – Belsky
The Blessed Church – Morris
Deep and Wide – Stanley
Visioneering – Stanley
Communicating for Change – Stanley
The Blessed Church – Morris
Who Stole My Church – MacDonald

Christian Life and Family Books

Revolutionary Parenting - Barna
Every Man's Battle – Arterburn
I Kissed Dating Goodbye – Harris
Boy Meets Girl – Harris
Choosing God's Best – Raunikar
The 5 Love Languages - Chapman
For Women Only – Feldhahn
For Men Only – Feldhahn
Sex Begins in the Kitchen - Lehman

Apologetics

More Than A Carpenter – McDowell
Evidence That Demands a Verdict - McDowell
The Case for Christ – Strobel
The Lie – Ham
More than Blind Faith - Walton

The following books by A.B. Simpson are available to download and read for free at:
https://www.cmalliance.org/resources/publications/

A larger Christian life
Service for the King
The Challenge of Missions
The Fourfold Gospel
The Gospel of Healing
The Lord for the Body
Walking in the Spirit
Wholly Sanctified

Did you know that you can send any pdf file to your kindle device? Here are the instructions if you're not sure how to do it.

http://www.amazon.com/gp/sendtokindle/email

Video Series
Anything by Beth Moore
Various resources by Kay Arthur
Apologetics by Josh MacDowell or Lee Strobel
Systematic Theology by R.C. Sproul
Various topics by Andy Stanley

I've also used videos from Answers in Genesis, as well as a number of sermons on Youtube and the Alliance website: cmalliance.org, as well as the videos on their Vimeo account.

ADDENDUM

QUESTIONING THIS DISCIPLESHIP PROCESS

I understand that anytime someone takes on an established practice or organization there will be a degree of pushback from those who have been operating within the established practices for years. This is natural. This can be a good thing – or it can be a bad thing. This can come from those who have been part of establishing the establishment or those who are afraid to scrutinize the process for fear that they'll find out that they were wrong. Rather than put up a front to fight something that can be a good change, prayerfully consider how you can be part of building into Christ's Kingdom – whether you use the old way or a new way.

The leaders of the established church at the time of Christ provided plenty of pushback for His comments to them, His scrutiny of their system, and His redefinition of God's interaction with man – as well as the church's role in that interaction. It was their job to scrutinize His claims, His criticism, and prayerfully ascertain if He was God and if His comments were to be heeded or dismissed. Some of them found that He was God, so He had the authority to say what He said and do what He did, and they submitted to His authority and worked to make the changes. Others dismissed His claims and refused to allow the Holy Spirit to speak to their hearts. They were the ones who arrested Him and crucified Him.

Let us live our lives in a manner in which we continually prayerfully consider what the Holy Spirit is saying to us, the changes He's calling us to make in our lives, and have the courage to respond by allowing Him to do His work in us and through us.

A mentor of mine once suggested a reason why many older men and women in the church are afraid of asking the tough questions about purpose and process in the church is because they're afraid to find out that they've been doing church wrong for most of their lives. For most of us, it's much easier to ignore the tough questions, or redouble our efforts in the hopes of seeing a positive return.

As hard as it is for us to do an honest assessment and as much courage as it takes for us to actually make changes, I'd rather find out that I was doing it wrong by seeing that changes we made brought us into a paradigm that was working better – rather than go to my grave frustrated over a system that isn't producing the results that we desire. It might not be that we were doing it wrong then, but that our culture has changed and that we have to find a better way to reach the lost and make disciples in this culture.

There are good things and bad things in any system of man. In fact, there is no perfect system of man! The important thing is that we're actively involved in a system that is successfully building the Kingdom and we're seeing the fruit of that work. We'll always be in a good place if we're engaging in listening prayer and following His leading, no matter where He leads us.

We're probably not going to get it right the first time. But as we pray, develop a plan, step out with the plan, pray again, assess, tweak the plan, step out with the plan, and repeat over and over again we'll eventually land in the place He wants us to be in.

Here are a few questions that I've been asked about this rationale and practical plan to make disciples who make more disciples. Perhaps these are some questions that are on your mind right now as well.

Does everyone have to do it this way?

No, everyone doesn't have to do it this way. I know there are other books on this topic available, as well as other "systems of discipleship" available. I've read some of the books. I've tried some of the systems. There is no complete book. There is no perfect system. The system that I've outlined in this book is a system that has worked for me and those I've discipled. It's been replicated and it continues to work very well for us. I suggest it to you. I recommend it to you. I give you full permission to tweak it as the Lord leads you. I give you full permission to break it down to its bare components and build it back up in a system that works for you. The important thing isn't that you use this system (**or any one system**) but that you are using a system that is fruitfully making disciples who are making more disciples.

Isn't the person doing the mentoring taking the place of the Holy Spirit?

My answer is a resounding, "I never want to take the place of the Holy Spirit in someone's life!" In fact, my entire plan is to join ***the working of the Holy Spirit*** by spending time in prayer, Bible study, exploring His leading in areas of practical application, and allowing Him to use this relationship to mold both teacher and student more into the image of Jesus Christ. Both mentor and student are desperately dependent on the Holy Spirit to teach and guide all along the way.

As a pastor, I have this same goal through my preaching, through my teaching, through leading small groups, through my counseling, through my writing, as I chat with people on the phone and on Facebook, and in every other interaction that I have with others. I want to join the work of the Holy Spirit to help Him mold people into the image of Jesus Christ.

This has proven to be a good tool to radically accelerate that process. That is why I use it in my own personal life and ministry and I encourage others to use it as well.

Why do one-on-one relationships have to be at the 400 level? Can't anyone be part of them?

I am willing to have a one-on-one discipleship relationship with anyone who is willing to meet with me under the dynamics that I've defined, but I have learned that students at the 300 and 400-levels are the best potential students for this kind of a discipleship program.

I have two answers for this question:

First, in my experience, most of the questions I'm going to receive while discipling those who are at the 100 and 200-level will be covered by the material that I'm already covering in 200 and 300-level opportunities, so I'm better off inviting them to be part of the existing programs rather than duplicating the material I'm already covering there. I ask them to join us in that context and invite them into the one-on-one dynamic if they have more questions or desire to go even deeper.

I find that quite often their participation at the 200 and 300-level opportunities answers their question and satisfies their desire for spiritual formation at those levels for this time in their lives. When they've demonstrated that they're ready to go to the next level, that's the best time for me to invite them into a one-on-one discipleship relationship.

Secondly, if they're not willing to attend a 200 or 300-level ministry I've found there's a reason behind their decision. If a person isn't willing to learn with others at those levels they're probably not going to put the time and effort into the one-on-one investment.

I've encountered a variety of reasons people do not want to be in the 200 or 300-level setting. Such as: they have a problem with someone else in the room, they have a hard time talking about personal things in public, they realize that their talk is much different than their walk, they really just want you to find biblical reasons to agree with their own personal opinions, and they want to protect their image of being a mature believer even if they're not really a mature believer. Any of these reasons will hinder them from learning from a mentor one-on-one.

I've found that 200 and 300-level groups are the best places to find those who are ready to go deeper in a one-on-one relationship. They are the ones who are always asking really good questions. They are the ones who seek to apply the principles you're covering in their daily lives. They are the ones who have regular attendance, do the homework, and invite others to be part of the group. Going deeper in a one-on-one discipleship relationship takes time and initiative. If we're not seeing this demonstrated in a classroom-like setting it will probably be hard to find in a one-on-one setting. If you invite them into a one-on-one setting and they're not willing to do the homework then you might not be investing your time as well as you could by working with those who are willing to do the work.

Don't you think that your expectations are too high?

My answer is, "No, not really – and yeah, sometimes they are." Don't tell anyone I said this, but, sometimes I relax my expectations based on the spiritual maturity of the person I'm meeting with. There, I said it. But I will also say that every time I have relaxed my expectations the fruit from my time meeting with someone has diminished as well. As I look at all of those I'm meeting with, an honest assessment is that those who are willing to meet my expectations are the ones who are experiencing the most spiritual fruit from the process. Those who ask me to lower my expectations don't experience as much fruit as those who are willing to rise up to my expectations for our time together.

Still, nobody is able to compare the fruit across the spectrum of those I'm meeting with but me. So, each and every one of the people I'm meeting with are seeing fruit in their own life, and are giving God the glory for the fruit they're experiencing. A plan to determine who I'm going to meet with and how high I am going to hold my expectations helps me to determine a plan to use my own time wisely. I only have so much time to meet with people one-on-one! If my time is filled up with those who are looking for low expectations, then those who are willing to meet the higher expectations will have to wait in line – or miss out on the fruit of this kind of a relationship. I'd rather meet with those who are willing to dig in deeper and let others meet with those who wish my expectations were lower.

How many people can one person disciple at a time?

This really depends on how much time you have available! As a pastor who has made this an important part of my plan for developing spiritual formation in the lives of those I'm leading, I've made one-on-one discipleship a priority in my schedule. Still, I'm only able to meet with about 15 people at a time! That means that each week I'm spending 15-20 hours meeting with people who are willing to meet with me for one hour every week or every two weeks.

I'm not sure how much time you have to dedicate to meeting with people, but you shouldn't invite others into this kind of a relationship with you unless you have the time to dedicate to them for the entire time you commit to! One of the nicest aspects of this kind of a discipleship plan is that the person doing the discipling doesn't have a lot of homework to do – no, the person who is being discipled has the homework. The person doing the discipling is more of a guide than a teacher.

Let me propose a couple of scenarios for you.

Scenario 1

I set one day aside for me to meet with others to disciple them. Let's say that I give 6 hours every Saturday to meet with people. I expect them to meet with me one-on-one for one hour every week. I schedule a 30 minute buffer in our meeting times so that I can unwind from one meeting, spend a few minutes in prayer, and mentally prepare for the next meeting. I'm long-winded and quite often go right up to the end of our hour together so I found that scheduling a buffer helps to keep me on schedule. My schedule would look like this:

Noon – Bob
1:30 – Fred
3:00 – Tim
4:30 – Seth

So, under this scenario, I can disciple 4 people. If we plan to meet once every other week, then I can disciple 8 people.

Scenario 2

I set aside enough time to meet with two people on two different nights of the week.

Monday
7:00 – Bob
8:30 – Fred

Wednesday
7:00 – Tim
8:30 – Seth

Here I am able to meet with the same 4 people. If we plan to meet once every other week, then I can disciple 8 people.

Scenario 3

I set aside one day of office hours to disciple people one-on-one.

Thursday
9:00 – Bob
10:30 – Fred
12:00 – Justin (we go to lunch together)
2:00 – Este
4:30 – Joshua
6:00 – Seth
7:30 – Tim

Here I am realistically able to meet with 7 people each week. If we meet every other week, then I can disciple 14 people.

Scenario 4

If I'm much more flexible with my schedule I can meet with people as they are available throughout the week.

Monday
11:00am – Tim
3:00pm - Este
7:00pm – Seth

Thursday
3:00- Vince

Friday
10:00am – Larry
Noon – Justin
6:00 – Joshua

Here I am able to disciple 7 people. I would have time to disciple others based on both their schedule and my availability. If one-on-one discipleship is a priority to me in my ministry as a pastor, and it is, then I will make the time to meet with as many people as possible on their schedule. Then, I fit in the rest of my pastoring duties around my discipling schedule.

One Last Scenario

Myself and one person make the commitment to meet together once per week – depending on when we're available that week. We meet together at church on Sunday morning and decide what day and time is going to work for us that week. The day and time will change from week to week, but we're still meeting each week.

I don't want you to think that you can't do this because you don't see yourself fitting into any of the above scenarios! Anyone can do this! Discipling one person is a great start. It's far better than not meeting with anyone at all. Once you see the fruit of your time meeting with one person then you're going to be willing to make adjustments to your schedule to meet with others.

Of course, I'd like to see you find one person you can learn from and one person you can teach. So, in this scenario, you're meeting with two people as you're able to meet with them each week and you're determined to make the time required to meet with both of them each and every week.

How can everyone fit in this structure?

My first thought is "Everyone can't fit into the structure if ***I'm the only one doing it!***" In other words, "I can't disciple the whole church one-on-one!" I only have enough time to meet with about 10-15 people at a time. Hopefully the church is developing a one-on-one discipleship culture – where elders, board members, ministry leaders, mature godly men and women are meeting with others to disciple them one-on-one. Then, as a team, we will be able to create a dynamic where more and more people from the church are invited into this structure.

It doesn't take many operating in this paradigm to be able to cover the entire church. In a church of 100, we just need ten or eleven who are willing to disciple eight others and the entire church is meeting with someone in a one-on-one relationship. Think about the spiritual formation that will take place if that happens!!! In my experience, the entire church will not be willing to meet on a one-on-one basis. So, if half the church is interested in this kind of a program (which I think would be a phenomenal percentage), a team of a pastor, four elders, and a couple of other mature disciples within the church could easily implement this program.

Or some could meet with more than others. An elder could meet with ten, the pastor is meeting with twelve, an older saint in the church is meeting with three, and a few ministry leaders are meeting with two or three each. Keep in mind that part of this idea is that at the end of your time together, you say, "Now, you go and do likewise!" This concept is continually developing more disciples who are trained to make more disciples. This isn't a design that becomes more taxing over time – it's a design that becomes less taxing over time! There will always be more people who need to be discipled and more people prepared to disciple others!

What if someone falls through the cracks?

Someone is probably going to fall through the cracks! Someone is going to get sick, someone is going to bail on the process, someone is going to forget about their appointment, someone is going to move out of town, someone is going to use the one-on-one discipleship time as a fellowship gathering, or someone is going to... you name it! It's inevitable! This is why oversight from the elders or ministry leaders is so crucial if you're striving to develop a disciple-making culture in your church or ministry. Leadership must be looking for the gaps and acting to fix the gaps as soon as they're noticed. Remember, the Holy Spirit is the one who is doing the work of spiritual formation in the hearts and lives of those who are part of this program. So, if the leadership are seeking signs of the Holy Spirit's work, and joining Him in that work, striving to develop a culture where His work will go on unhindered, we can trust that the Holy Spirit will lead and direct the right way every time.

WORKS CITED

Chan, Francis, and Platt, David. *Don't Be Deceived, Disciples Make Disciples.*
https://www.youtube.com/watch?v=n6aqT7MOXo0

Dunbar's Number – Article on Wikipedia
https://en.wikipedia.org/wiki/Dunbar%27s_number

Engel, James. *What's Gone Wrong with the Harvest.* Grand Rapids: Zondervan, 1975.

Huff Post, Poll: 28 Percent Of Americans Have Not Read A Book In The Past Year. 10-7-2003, http://www.huffingtonpost.com/2003/10/07/american-read-book-poll_n_4045937.html

Mulholland, Robert. *Invitation to a Journey: A Road Map for Spiritual Formation*. Downers Grove: Inter Varsity Press, 1993.

Reeves, Thomas. "Not So Christian America". 1996.
http://www.firstthings.com/article/1996/10/001-not-so-christian-america

Spader, Dan, and Mayes, Gary. *Growing a Healthy Church.* Chicago: Moody Publishers, 1991.

http://www.sermoncentral.com/pastors-preaching-articles/kara-powell-the-research-is-in-this-is-the-1-reason-students-leave-the-church-2261.asp

ABOUT THE AUTHOR

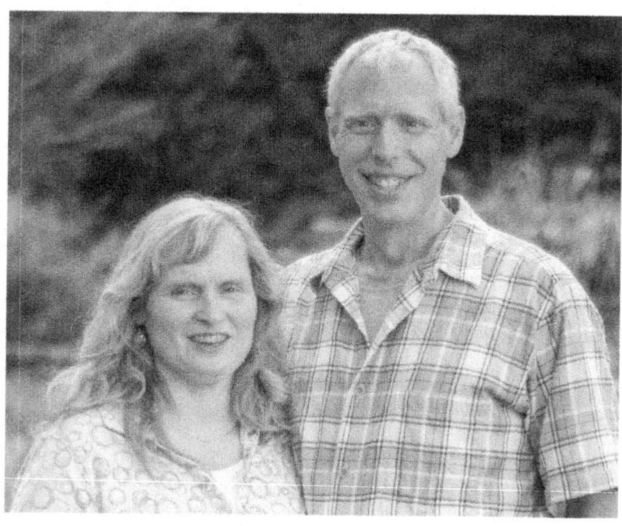

PJ (Pastor Jim) Bogoniewski, and his wife, Sandra, have four amazing kids of their own. As they've lived their lives missionally, the Lord has led them to "adopt" four others as older teenagers and young adults. Sandra has dedicated her life to raising and homeschooling their four children. PJ worked as a draftsman, writer, editor, and desktop publisher before entering full-time ministry with the Christian and Missionary Alliance as a second career in 2002.

In addition to books about deeper Christian living, PJ has written dozens of plays that are designed to creatively convey biblical truths in a church, or a Christian school, setting.

You will find a complete list of PJ's writings by visiting his Acts of Light ministry website:

www.ActsofLight.com

You can also download study questions for this book to use in personal or group study for free at the Acts of Light website.

This title is also available in electronic format on Kindle
and available in audible format on Audible.
You can find more information on all titles and formats at:
www.ActsofLight.com

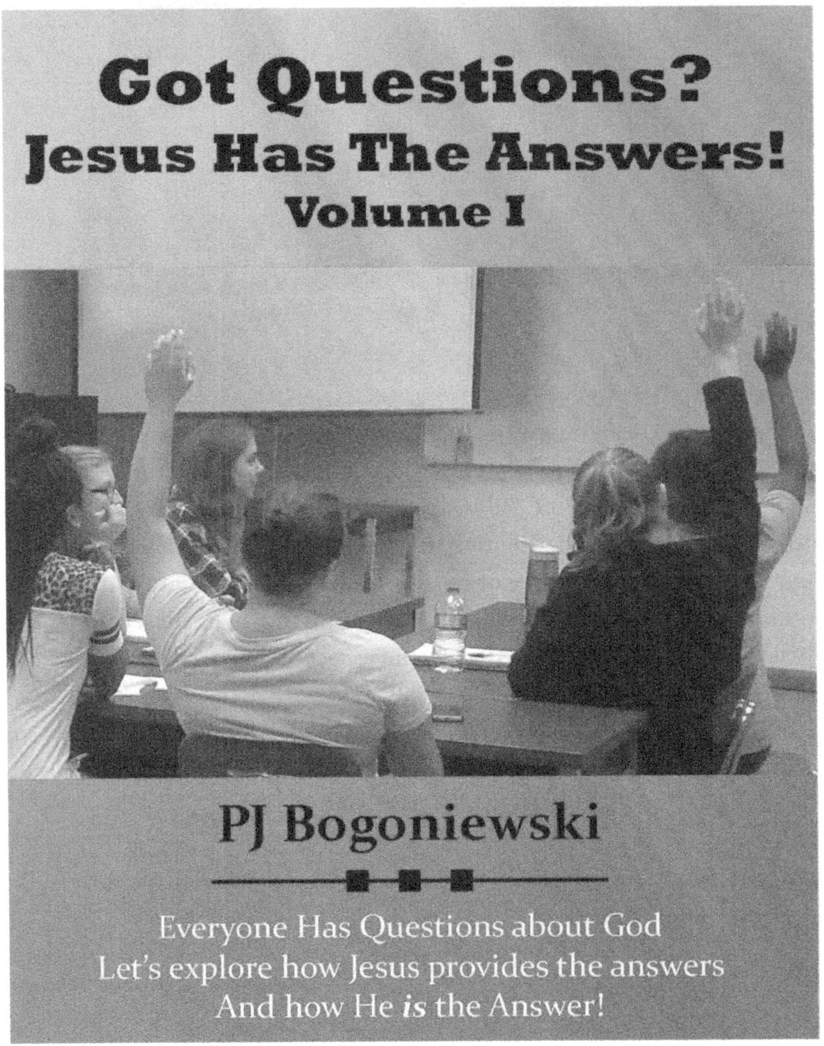

This title is also available in electronic format on Kindle
and available in audible format on Audible.
You can find more information on all titles and formats at:
www.ActsofLight.com

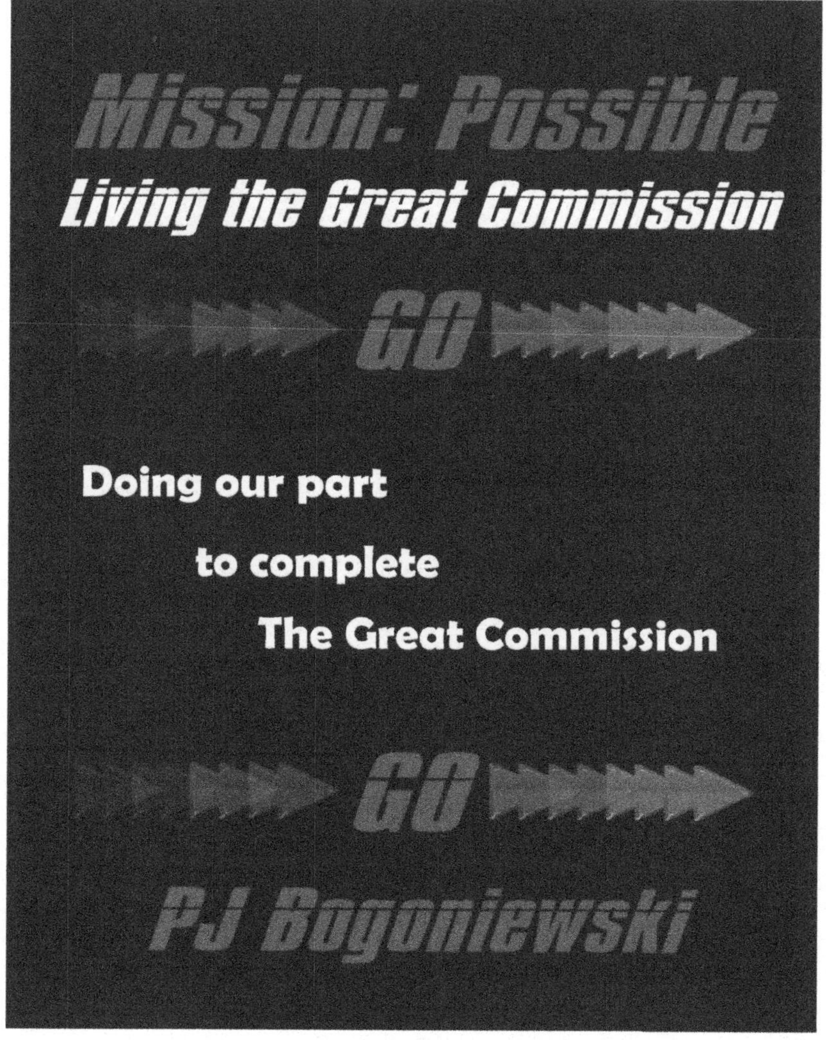

Made in the USA
Monee, IL
16 January 2024

51163781R00134